Wealth and Homeownership

Mariacristina Rossi • Eva M. Sierminska

Wealth and Homeownership

Women, Men and Families

Mariacristina Rossi
Department of Management, School of
Management and Economics
University of Torino
Torino, Italy

Eva M. Sierminska
LISER - Luxembourg Institute of
Socio-Economic Research
Esch-Belval, Luxembourg

ISBN 978-3-319-92557-8   ISBN 978-3-319-92558-5 (eBook)
https://doi.org/10.1007/978-3-319-92558-5

Library of Congress Control Number: 2018943399

© The Editor(s) (if applicable) and The Author(s) 2018
This work is subject to copyright. All rights are solely and exclusively licensed by the Publisher, whether the whole or part of the material is concerned, specifically the rights of translation, reprinting, reuse of illustrations, recitation, broadcasting, reproduction on microfilms or in any other physical way, and transmission or information storage and retrieval, electronic adaptation, computer software, or by similar or dissimilar methodology now known or hereafter developed.
The use of general descriptive names, registered names, trademarks, service marks, etc. in this publication does not imply, even in the absence of a specific statement, that such names are exempt from the relevant protective laws and regulations and therefore free for general use.
The publisher, the authors, and the editors are safe to assume that the advice and information in this book are believed to be true and accurate at the date of publication. Neither the publisher nor the authors or the editors give a warranty, express or implied, with respect to the material contained herein or for any errors or omissions that may have been made. The publisher remains neutral with regard to jurisdictional claims in published maps and institutional affiliations.

Cover illustration: Abstract Bricks and Shadows © Stephen Bonk/Fotolia.co.uk

This Palgrave Pivot imprint is published by the registered company Springer Nature Switzerland AG
The registered company address is: Gewerbestrasse 11, 6330 Cham, Switzerland

The journey of a thousand miles begins with one step.
—Lao Tzu

To Our Dads

Foreword

Interest in household finances amongst both academics and policymakers has been steadily growing over the past two to three decades. Furthermore, the global financial crisis highlighted the financial vulnerability faced by many households holding high levels of debt yet low, or even no, financial assets to draw upon in times of economic adversity. This book makes a valuable contribution to knowledge related to one of the key financial assets held by households, namely, their house—a financial asset, which provides shelter as well as serves as an important long-term financial investment. This timely book provides a comprehensive analysis of this complex dual characteristic of housing as both a consumption and an investment good. Furthermore, the detailed cross-country comparisons presented highlight the importance of the institutional context faced by households, as well as the implications of the changing welfare state. Such changes are related to the repeated warnings of a future pension crisis likely to be faced by many households who are not saving enough to safeguard their financial future in retirement. This book thus, provides a timely reminder of the role of homeownership as a means to provide financial security later on in life, as well as the complex interaction between decisions regarding the holding of liquid and illiquid financial assets. Indeed, the nature of the portfolio of assets held at the household level has important implications for financial security in the face of potential shocks to health and employment, as well as for long-term financial planning.

The focus on gender and the changing nature of families provides a crucial context relating to the financial decision-making processes at play. Whilst issues related to the gender pay gap are rightly raised by the media, academia and policymakers, the gender wealth gap has attracted much less attention. This book places such issues related to wealth at the center of the analysis and debate. There are many reasons why such issues are important from a gender perspective including single families and the longer life expectancy of women relative to men. Indeed, the discussion on the changing nature of families presented in this book sheds light on this crucial, yet often overlooked, aspect of household finances. Thus, understanding the decision processes that lie behind wealth accumulation and homeownership are fundamentally important in understanding the gender wealth gap. Indeed, a related area covered by the book relates to the role played by financial knowledge and literacy, which in turn influence attitudes toward risk and risk aversion, thereby having important implications for financial decision making and inequalities in wealth.

At a time when young people are struggling to get a foot on the housing ladder in many countries and important decisions are made by young people regarding both financial and human capital investments, this book fills a crucial gap in our knowledge related to an asset, which some members of the older generations may take for granted, yet for some members of the younger generations, ownership of this asset appears somewhat aspirational and out of reach. This book is essential reading for anyone interested in household finances, an area which I have been researching since 2005. It provides insightful analysis of past research and important topical issues, as well as, highlights avenues to focus on in the future, and, in my opinion, will serve to stimulate further research and interest in the ever-growing literature on household finance.

Sheffield, UK   Sarah Brown

Preface

The importance of wealth has become more and more central in shaping households' welfare. Particularly nowadays with the shrinking of welfare states and public pension provisions, private wealth can represent an important resource to draw upon in order to maintain the standards of living at the desired level after retirement. When looking at wealth and its composition, housing (principal residence, in particular) stands out as the biggest portion of wealth. In almost every country, wealth is predominantly constituted by housing equity. Thus, looking at wealth while ignoring housing would be seen as a contradiction.

Many books have been written on wealth; we ourselves have taken part in some research projects on wealth accumulation and its impact on household welfare and economic decisions. What has not been written yet is a book that sets the conceptual stage on these topics (wealth and housing) and provides a cross-national picture of wealth outcomes in this dimension for families (using newly available data) to be used by scholars, students and policymakers. The differences between women and men in wealth accumulation have been even more seldomly discussed.

The idea of this book was to merge together what both of us have been working on for many years: the rationale behind wealth accumulation and the empirical outcomes. In other words, our goal has been to emphasize our expertise on wealth empirical analysis, with sound conceptual background to interpret the results.

In this book, we investigate the link between wealth and housing, the latter being a quite complicated decision per se. We begin the book by providing a conceptual framework within which the process of wealth accumulation and homeownership can be examined. We use this framework throughout the book.

Next, we discuss the importance of studying wealth and housing wealth more generally and focus on the variation across countries. We also discuss why families and women and men in particular may differ in the way they accumulate wealth. Some methodological issues that accompany wealth studies are also pointed out.

Chapter 3 follows homeownership trends in the developed world with a regional focus across families and elaborates on the determinants of homeownership.

The final chapter investigates whether homeownership is associated with higher wealth levels, using regression analysis along with descriptive statistics. Despite not claiming causality, homeownership is associated with higher wealth. We conclude the chapter by pointing to possible drawbacks of wealth accumulation especially via housing equity. An excessively illiquid portfolio can act as a vulnerability effect, especially at old age.

The book finishes by highlighting some of the potential drawbacks for families of having excessive levels of housing wealth.

Creating this book was a lengthy process and we are grateful to everyone who helped us along the way, either directly or indirectly via inspiration. We would also like to thank the institutions LISER for supporting our work and the LIS datacenter for providing invaluable access and insights to the data.

Torino, Italy   Mariacristina Rossi
Esch-Belval, Luxembourg   Eva M. Sierminska

Acknowledgments

I wish to thank my father, Zygmunt, for planting the seed of a linear need of accomplishment and being my rock no matter what; Alik and Emil—Alik for being my sweetness and reminding me I am the "mommy," and Emil for being my baby—always—with flawless logic and determination; and my honey M. for being there, for supporting me during the storms as well as the long sunny days. It's been a great adventure. I also wish to thank the rest of my family for numerous gestures and acts of support. This book would not have come to be without my dear circle of friends and colleagues located all over the world, who have in some way contributed to who I am and in what direction I am headed. I am greatly humbled to have you in my life.

—Eva

Finally, we would like to thank each other for our great bravery that led us to embark on this journey, a journey that started in a café in Turin in Piazza Madama Cristina in 2013.

Contents

1 Introduction and Conceptual Framework 1

2 Wealth Variation Across Countries 19

3 Families and Housing Decisions: A Look Across OECD Countries 55

4 Homeownership and Wealth Accumulation 93

Concluding Remarks 117

Index 119

List of Figures

Fig. 1.1 Consumption, Income and Asset over the Life Cycle 9

Fig. 2.1 Median net worth across selected countries (in 2011 USD). Source: Luxembourg Income Study (LIS) data (AU, AT, CA, FI, GR, IT, UK and US) and Household Finance and Consumption Survey (HFCS) (BE, DE, ES, FR, LU, NL). Note: *AU* Australia; *AT* Austria; *CA* Canada; *FI* Finland; *GR* Greece; *IT* Italy; *UK* United Kingdom and *US* United States; *BE* Belgium; *DE* Germany; *ES* Spain; *FR* France; *LU* Luxembourg; *NL* the Netherlands 30

Fig. 2.2 Median net worth by family types across selected countries (in 2011 USD). Source: LIS data (AU, AT, CA, FI, GR, IT, UK and US) and HFCS (BE, DE, ES, FR, LU, NL). Note: *AU* Australia; *AT* Austria; *CA* Canada; *FI* Finland; *GR* Greece; *IT* Italy; *UK* United Kingdom and *US* United States; *BE* Belgium; *DE* Germany; *ES* Spain; *FR* France; *LU* Luxembourg; *NL* the Netherlands 34

Fig. 2.3 Median net worth by age across selected countries (in 2011 USD). Source: LIS data (AU, AT, CA, FI, GR, IT, UK and US) and HFCS (BE, DE, ES, FR, LU, NL). Note: *AU* Australia; *AT* Austria; *CA* Canada; *FI* Finland; *GR* Greece; *IT* Italy; *UK* United Kingdom and *US* United States; *BE* Belgium; *DE* Germany; *ES* Spain; *FR* France; *LU* Luxembourg; *NL* the Netherlands 36

List of Figures

Fig. 2.4	Median net worth by age and family type across selected countries (in 2011 USD). Source: LIS data (AU, AT, CA, FI, GR, IT, UK and US) and HFCS (BE, DE, ES, FR, LU, NL). Note: *AU* Australia; *AT* Austria; *CA* Canada; *FI* Finland; *GR* Greece; *IT* Italy; *UK* United Kingdom and *US* United States; *BE* Belgium; *DE* Germany; *ES* Spain; *FR* France; *LU* Luxembourg; *NL* the Netherlands	37
Fig. 3.1	Homeownership rates by country for women and men household heads. Source: LIS data; own calculations	63
Fig. 3.2	Homeownership rates by family type across decades (for singles and singles with kids). Source: LIS data; own elaboration	64
Fig. 3.3	Homeownership rates across different cohorts of female household heads. Source: LIS data; own calculations	72
Fig. 3.4	Homeownership by gender of the household head. Source: LIS data; own calculations	84
Fig. 3.5	Homeownership rates by family type over the decades (for married and married with kids). Source: LIS data; own elaboration	85
Fig. 4.1	Homeownership rate in Europe by family types	102
Fig. 4.2	Age and average (log) wealth by status	103

List of Tables

Table 2.1	Median net worth and ratio over total by family types across selected countries (in 2011 USD)	31
Table 2.2	Average value of principal residence, total assets and home equity across selected countries (in 2011 USD)	39
Table 2.3	Principal residence and home equity as a share of total assets and percent of principal residence owned outright across countries (in 2011 USD)	41
Table 3.1	Homeownership rates and changes over time	61
Table 3.2	Homeownership probit estimates for the pooled sample of waves (marginal effects)	67
Table 3.3	Homeownership probit estimated for the pooled sample of waves for the cohort of 25–45 years old (marginal effects)	74
Table 3.4	Homeownership probit estimates for the pooled sample of waves for the cohort of 45–65 years old (marginal effects)	78
Table 3.5	Data availability in our selected countries in the LIS database	86
Table 3.6	Variables used in the estimation	86
Table 3.7	LIS datacenter source surveys	87
Table 3.8	Household structure across countries by waves	88
Table 4.1	Family types, homeownership and net wealth	101
Table 4.2	Net Wealth regressions by country	103
Table 4.3	Net Wealth regression (pooled sample)	104
Table 4.4	Determinants of wealth (log)	106

1

Introduction and Conceptual Framework

Abstract This chapter introduces the reader to the key variables of our book: wealth and homeownership. We first briefly describe the evolution of assets and homeownership and then provide a conceptual framework within which the decision process of wealth accumulation and homeownership can be examined. This framework will be used as the conceptual background used to interpret asset accumulation decisions.

Keywords Intertemporal • Life Cycle Permanent Income Hypothesis

1.1 Introduction

Wealth differs widely across countries. It is six times higher than income in the US and shows similar values in several European countries, peaking at 700% of national income in Belgium (OECD data portal 2014). Wealth is a stock variable, which means that it is the sum of the flow of savings over the years and received bequest. In other words, considering that it is the sum of past choices, it is inevitably difficult to consistently change its value and particularly at an older age. For this reason, the importance of the pace of wealth accumulation at a young age is particularly important as little can be done to change the savings buffer stock when retirement approaches—which is when wealth is mostly needed. Lower saving rates over the years can generate enormous differences in the accumulation process. Given this feature, while it is reasonable to expect that people can change habits and become, for example, more parsimonious, it is unlikely that wealth level will be consistently impacted if the change in habit is not permanent.

The level of wealth is built up over the lifetime; very little can be done to reverse a wealth trend later in life. On the one side, the accumulation pattern over the lifetime, also known as saving propensity, will determine the amount of wealth a household can dispose of at retirement. On the other side, inheritance can give an important shape to wealth during one's lifetime, without depending on the saving attitude of a household. As highlighted by the recent work of Piketty (2014), inheritance of the baby boom generations, who have accumulated unprecedented levels of wealth, will pass to the next generation and shape the future social and economic equilibria. At the same time, self-made fortunes will also play an important role in this process (Kopczuk 2015).

In some countries, wealth prosperity is not aligned with GDP country rankings, showing divergence in performance. However, wealth is probably the best summary measure of potential income for the elderly, particularly if they cannot rely on generous pension systems like it has been the case in the past. Wealth can roughly represent future incomes available when divided by the expected remaining years in life, in the absence of other incomes.

In most countries, one of the main components of assets is housing equity. It has gained importance over recent decades, as easier and cheaper access to mortgage credit in the financial markets became available. Real estate is now fully recognized as one of the main drivers of economic fluctuations, as well as financial markets in economies with developed financial systems. Housing wealth accounts for almost half of net wealth in the UK, a little less in the US and more than 50% in most of the European countries (Muellbauer 2008). As a term of comparison, housing wealth is twice the size of pension wealth in the UK. Given the magnitude of wealth tied to (owner-occupied) housing wealth, home-owning households are inevitably exposed to fluctuations in real market prices.

As is discussed in Chap. 3, homeownership has increased steadily over the years and has now reached around 70% in European countries and the US (Angelini et al. 2013), with Germany and Switzerland being the only exceptions, where roughly 50% or less are homeowners. Homeownership represents the basis for a number of positive outcomes, not only social and economic, but also health outcomes, as well as civic and psychological attitudes among others.[1]

Focusing on the positive economic outcomes associated with owning your own home, changes in wealth are cited as the most important consequence of homeownership (Dietz and Haurin 2003), and homeownership is considered to be a good predictor of total wealth. Several studies have proven that this is actually the case, and a strong correlation exists between homeownership and wealth levels in the US, as well as in EU countries (Bricker et al. 2012; Sierminska 2012). We study this in more detail in Chap. 4.

For the majority of people, the capital tied up in their primary (and most of the time, only) residence constitutes their entire wealth. Housing is seen as a vehicle to accumulate assets as it fosters an orientation toward the future (Sherraden 1991) and can, as a result, turn into a higher rate of wealth accumulation than in the case of renting. Homeownership also generates an additional implicit commitment to save, which increases the wealth of homeowners, either because they are committed through a mortgage scheme or because they have a consistent amount of wealth tied into illiquid wealth. They cannot dispose of this wealth in the same way they could do were they renting and owning an equivalent asset. As a consequence, being a homeowner exacerbates the saving propensity. Homeownership could also have an impact on wealth inequality as well. This channel is investigated and has proven to be at work in a recent study by Kindermann and Kohls (2017).

In our book, we aim to investigate whether different types of households and the gender dimension are associated with different shapes of homeownership and wealth. If this is the case, this could potentially provide different profiles of wealth accumulation solely based on household composition. Why a look at gender in a discussion on wealth accumulation? A lot has been written on the participation of women in the labor market. Access to the labor market represents the first channel to increasing female participation in the society with an active role. Earning a salary in the market is the first step in the independence ladder. Labor market indicators and the gap between women and men in employment opportunities and salaries is the first measurement tool policy-makers look at when they assess female participation in economic life.

Without disregarding this fundamental step, we turn our focus to another understudied element of economic life: wealth. Wealth is a stock, and thus reflects the history of past events. If for young generations (net) wealth can be irrelevant or even negative, for households approaching retirement wealth can constitute a substantial amount of income. The importance of wealth, relative to income, is thus much stronger.

What drives wealth accumulation? What are the ingredients of wealth, and why should women differ from men in wealth formation?

When we think of wealth, we think of a household decision related to its accumulation. However, the term *household* is difficult to define. In many household surveys, a household is defined as one or more individuals living in the same dwelling and sharing at least three meals together. The household is considered the unit of economic analysis, as it is composed of a group of individuals acting as one person once they make joint economic decisions (Rossi 2008; Rossi and Trucchi 2016). As described in more detail in Chap. 2, household types vary widely. Households experience life events and change over time: kids' birth, separation, and/or widowhood are all part of the life process. Households can be a couple or single person with or without children. Potentially, each type differs in their wealth decision-making process. Standard models of savings and consumption decisions refer to the household as a one-person household. Traditionally, the man was the main earner, and financial planning was implicitly associated with "him." As explained in the next section, the basic model to interpret the life cycle is for a one income earner household; in the past this was usually a man. Nowadays with two-earner households being more prevalent, financial decisions can be either the outcome of a common decision process or the decision of the financially responsible person. Women with their more visible presence in the labor market are playing a more important role in the household budget. Does this have an impact on wealth decisions?[2]

Traditionally, men were more involved in the investment decisions, without female spouses necessarily knowing the portfolio investments managed by the husband (Rossi and Sierminska 2015). In the US, only about 15% of women handle their household's investments. If the spouse handling the investment passes away first, this creates a lot of financial instability for the surviving spouse who is likely to be female—given that a woman is twice as likely to live longer than her husband (Marrella 2014). Thus, a vast majority of women, despite having a considerable amount of wealth, can be unprepared for handling it. In addition, affluent women are on the rise, despite the slow pace at which access to the top position is gained. The new lifestyle of affluent women is calling for a new approach on how to assist them regarding financial advice, following their needs and interests.

In the last chapter of this book, we investigate whether homeownership is associated with higher wealth, using an econometric analysis on European microdata, albeit the relationship cannot be claimed to be causal. Being a homeowner is. In fact, homeownership is a decision in itself, which is, in turn, driven by a higher propensity for accumulation. Finding a positive association between homeownership and wealth could just be capturing the propensity for accumulation of the household, making the causality claim difficult to prove.

In addition, we add some reflections on the potential for negative consequences of excessive accumulation in housing, which, as will be shown, can generate excessively illiquid portfolio levels.

1.2 The Economic Rationale of Wealth Accumulation

By deciding what to devote to today's consumption versus tomorrow's consumption (savings), households make one of the most important decisions regarding their income. According to the standard Economic

Theory, this is done by choosing the best outcome given their preferences, structured over the life cycle as follows (Deaton 1992):

$$\max_{c_1...c_T} U(c_1,,c_2,,...c_T) = \max_{c_1...c_T} u(c_1)$$
$$+u(c_2)\frac{1}{1+\delta}+...+u(c_T)\frac{1}{(1+\delta)^{T-1}}. \tag{1.1}$$

Preferences are time separable, which, in simple words, means that households benefit from what they consume each period, without being affected by what happened in previous periods. Were households affected by previous consumption levels, they would exhibit habit formation or durability—depending on whether past consumption levels decrease the current utility, as in the case of habit, or they enhance it, as in the case of durability (Alessie and Lusardi 1997; Dynan 2000; Guariglia and Rossi 2002). Moreover, in the simplest formulation, leisure does not enter the utility function, which means the amount of leisure time does not count and only consumption generates utility. It is worth noting that wealth per se does not enter directly in the utility function, as only consumption gives utility. Empirical analysis has, instead, highlighted how net wealth and the level of indebtedness are an important determinant of subjective well-being (Brown and Gray 2016). Moreover, social values such as social goods or social investments do not enter in the traditional utility function, which means that people would never invest in a lower than the market return investment as they do not maximize utility. The empirical evidence shows, in contrast, that people donate or invest in an asset lower than the market return by deriving utility from non-monetary return (Rossi et al. 2018; Gambardella et al. 2018). Including non-monetary elements in the utility function would make the modeling more aligned with actual behavior.

The attitude toward savings and, hence, consumption, as well as risk attitudes, can also be driven by habits formed in adolescence and childhood as shown by Brown and Taylor (2016) for Britain.

Subject to the period by period budget constraint:

$$A_t = A_{t-1}(1+r) + y_t - c_t, \quad (1.2)$$

where r stands for interest rate, δ for the subjective discount rate, for which individuals get less utility if they consume the same amount of goods one year later. A stands for assets and y for income. Supposing that initial and terminal wealth are zero, which is equivalent to saying that inheritances and bequests are set to zero, we can rewrite the budgets as one unique intertemporal budget[3]:

$$c_1 + \frac{c_2}{(1+r)} + \ldots + \frac{c_T}{(1+r)^{T-1}} = y_1 + \frac{y_2}{(1+r)} + \ldots + \frac{y_T}{(1+r)^{T-1}}. \quad (1.3)$$

1.2.1 Consumption

Solving this constrained optimization problem,[4] we can obtain the optimal value of consumption, constant over time, as such:

$$c^* = \frac{r}{(1+r)\left(1-(1+r)^{-T}\right)} \sum_{1}^{T} \frac{y_i}{(1+r)^{i-1}}. \quad (1.4)$$

For T tending to infinity, it follows that consumption is the permanent income, that is, the annuity value of the discounted value of future income flow (Friedman 1957), according to the following rule:

$$c^* = \frac{r}{(1+r)} \sum_{1}^{\infty} \frac{y_i}{(1+r)^{i-1}} \quad (1.5)$$

Optimal consumption will determine the optimal value of the stock variable—wealth. It is useful to remind the reader that assets per se do not give utility to households, but they are rather an ancillary tool to reach the optimal consumption path.

The value of wealth at each year is then determined by substituting optimal consumption Eq. (1.4) in the budget Eq. (1.3). For example, in period one, wealth is equal to:

$$A_1 = y_1 \frac{r(1+r)^T}{(1+r)^{T+1}-1} - \frac{r}{(1+r)\left(1-(1+r)^{-T}\right)} \sum_{2}^{T} \frac{y_i}{(1+r)^{i-1}}. \quad (1.6)$$

According to this model, two households with equal discounted income flows and equal preferences will exhibit the same consumption, but potentially be different in wealth terms if income is timed differently among the two. As an extreme example, consider one household receiving one income (Y) at period one and another household receiving the same amount of income $-Y(1 + r)^T$—the last year. Lifetime income is identical and so is consumption, but assets will show an opposite path. Evaluating the vulnerability of a household by solely looking at assets would be terribly misleading; indeed, the two households have the same living standards in terms of income, but show opposite profiles of wealth.

1.2.2 Savings

It is worth noticing that wealth is likely to be negative in the first years of the life cycle given that future incomes are likely to be increasing. At a young age, individuals are likely to show negative net wealth as they borrow against their future (higher income). The process of savings is instead related to negative future income changes, the so-called saving for a *rainy day* (Deaton 1992). To show why savings predict bad future income prospects, let us use the formula for optimal savings, which is derived by plugging the value of consumption in Eq. (1.4) into the budget Eq. (1.2). The value of savings in t, thus, is as follows:

$$s_t = -E_t \frac{y_{t+1}-y_t}{1+r} - \frac{y_{t+2}-y_{t+1}}{(1+r)^2} - \ldots$$

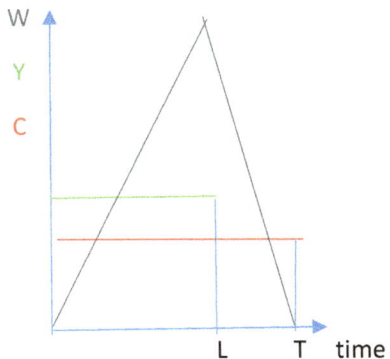

Fig. 1.1 Consumption, Income and Asset over the Life Cycle

Saving is then the sum of discounted future income changes, with the reverse sign. Indeed, people save if they predict future drops in income, while they dissave or borrow if their future incomes are on average higher than the current one. In the nutshell example provided by Modigliani and Brumberg (1954), people save before retirement as their current income is above the average lifetime income. Dissaving will start at retirement and will continue, as illustrated in Fig. 1.1. Negative future income prospects should rationally increase savings. Brown and Taylor (2016) show that this effect could also be at work at the intergenerational level; children of optimistic parents show a lower probability of savings by approximately 2 percentage points.

Drawing from the seminal work of Modigliani and Brumberg (1954), the well-known stripped-down life cycle formula for consumption and wealth can be illustrated in the graph in Fig. 1.1.

As illustrated in Fig. 1.1, this is the simplest version of income profiles, which are constant (equal to Y) over the working life (lasting L years) and then drop to zero after retirement. Retirement lasts until the end of life (happening with certainty at time T).[5] In the simplest assumption of zero interest rate, consumption is just the ratio between total lifetime resources ($L*Y$) and life length (T), as follows:

$$c = \frac{YL}{T}. \quad (1.7)$$

Equation (1.6) is the stripped-down version of Eq. (1.4), where the interest rate is set to zero and income is constant at level Y. The household compatible with that model is a single-earner household, which is probably less adequate to be representative of the family working structure most prevalent nowadays.

The basic intuition of the life cycle model carries out the role of personal wealth as the first form of self-made pension wealth: people accumulate to face lifetimes at zero income. Income dropping to zero after working life excludes the presence of a pension system, where net income during the working life is reduced by pension contributions, which will be returned as pension benefits after retirement occurs. A pension system "replaces" personal savings, as it generates pension wealth via mandatory savings rather than leaving individuals free to decide their optimal accumulation. The higher the intensity of contribution into the pension system, the lower the private saving, ceteris paribus (Rossi 2009).

1.2.3 Borrowing Constraints

If borrowing were not restricted, the introduction of a pension system would be neutral. However, in a more realistic setting, the financial system does not allow one to borrow freely to accomplish the optimal consumption plan. The inability to borrow as desired (i.e. to follow the optimal plan) is known as "liquidity or borrowing constraint."

Formally this can be summarized with a simple inequality as follows:

$$A_t \geq -B,$$

stating that assets (A) cannot be lower by a fixed threshold equal to B at any time t. As an example, if families are allowed to borrow at most €1000, assets have to be higher than minus €1000. The most restricted example of the existence of borrowing constraints is when any borrowing is impeded, by making B equal to zero.

The existence of liquidity constraints will inevitably change the profile of achievable consumption for those households who would need to borrow to achieve their consumption pattern (such as those households at young ages whose income profile is rapidly increasing over time).

As a consequence of the life cycle and borrowing restrictions, country asset levels should be strongly related to age (assets following an inverse U-shaped curve as illustrated in Fig. 1.1), and positively correlated with credit restrictions. Having little or no access to credit, indeed, will force the young cohort to oversave (or under-indebting), which, in turn, will generate a higher saving rate compared to countries where access to credit is less restricted. In our empirical analysis, carried out in Chaps. 3 and 4, we take into account macro effects, such as access to credit at the country level.

1.2.4 Precautionary Savings

Another element not yet mentioned that could potentially explain accumulation is the presence of uncertainty. So far, households are supposed to live in a certain world. If life uncertainty can be neutralized by buying life insurance, income uncertainty represents an uninsurable risk (at least partially). One of the risks that is impossible to neutralize completely by subscribing an insurance is indeed unemployment risk (Deaton 1992).[6] Income uncertainty generates additional savings, due to the precautionary motives, by enhancing the accumulation process (Guariglia 2001; Mishra et al. 2012; Rossi and Sansone 2017). Intuitively, despite offering the same expected income profiles, a noisier environment will induce prudent individuals to overaccumulate with respect to the case of perfect certainty, which has been shown in Sect. 1.2.

1.3 Portfolio Choice: The Role of Housing

In the previous description of the asset accumulation process (Sect. 1.2), we have not yet discussed housing. Indeed, housing, which is one of the most important investment decisions in a lifetime, is a difficult "ingredient" to think of in the rational decision of the household.

Housing is both an investment and a consumption good, which means that it generates utility for the service that it provides to the household. Calling h the housing service (say squared meters), we can think of the utility of a household at each year being represented by the following:

$$u(c_t, h_t) \qquad (1.8)$$

While the budget constraint for a homeowner will include the cost of housing, which has been bought at the price p_t at time t. If the household is a renter, the price paid each year is r_t, which is the rental price.

It is important to stress that what gives utility to households is the housing service, rather than whether the dwelling is owned. Hence, two households living in identical apartments would generate the same utility to households, irrespective of whether the dwelling is owned or not. In equilibrium, there should be no difference in owing or renting; had one choice dominated another, there would be room for price adjustment until the point where the two choices are equivalent.

Buying a house is part of the portfolio investment and constitutes a risky asset (unlike bonds that are defined as risk-free assets) since housing values are known at purchase but unknown at sale. Like any other risky investment, housing increases the importance that price fluctuations might have on household welfare; however, unlike any other investment, it generates utility as described above, the term h in the utility function in Eq. (1.8) (Chetty et al. 2017).

1.4 The Role of Bequests in Asset Accumulation

The role of housing can be even more peculiar compared to other assets when bequests are taken into consideration. Bequests are often in the form of housing, especially in Southern Mediterranean countries, as shown by Romiti and Rossi (2014). If households plan to bequeath to their children, accumulating resources in real estate, which the household inhabits, can be the ideal way to do this. Indeed, saving into housing equity is easier than saving in other assets, as housing generates, as we have already discussed, direct utility through housing services.

Bequests do not enter in the traditional life cycle model as illustrated in Sect. 1.2, as individuals are assumed to get utility only from their own consumption. However, if individuals are altruistic, following the original altruism model provided by Becker (1974), their utility function is directly affected by the well-being of their offspring or other people they care about. The larger the amount of wealth transmitted to their heirs, the larger the utility of the current household. This twist radically changes the life cycle view according to which terminal wealth is postulated to be null. Instead, the fact that people die with consistent amount of assets can be reconciled with strong bequest motives among altruistic parents (see, among others, Coda Moscarola et al. 2012).

The theoretical framework explaining the rationale of wealth accumulation is sound and extensive. Indeed, the empirical evidence shows partial alignment to the theoretical implications of the Life Cycle Permanent Income (LCPI) model. Better investigations on what actually drives household decisions regarding savings and wealth accumulations remain open for future research agendas.

1.5 Conclusion

Wealth is a key factor in understanding household welfare particularly nowadays, when wealth is at unprecedented levels in OECD countries and will be transmitted to the next generation. Particularly for older people, wealth is a good approximation of well-being. Indeed, wealth can be transformed in a flow of incomes that top up pension incomes, by determining the consumption level, and, as a consequence, the welfare level achievable by households.

In this chapter, we provide the tools to conceptualize wealth accumulation patterns, which respond to the optimality plans of families. Wealth is, however, an ancillary variable to the optimal consumption pattern, which generates utility to the household. It hence follows that decumulation should start to happen at some point of the life cycle as assets generate no utility after death. Accumulation of wealth is per se a positive thing as households are less vulnerable to the realizations of bad shocks, when they are able to rely on asset buffer stock. Conversely, excessive accumulation, especially if embedded into housing, could generate vulnerability for the household.

Housing, unlike bonds, is a peculiar form asset that also gives utility per se to the household, by providing housing services. In this chapter, we also provide the conceptual background for housing portfolio decisions, albeit this topic has much less theoretical consensus in the literature. Housing is both a consumption good and an investment good; thus in the next chapters, we will concentrate on investigating the empirical evidence of both on the determinants of homeownership and on the amount of wealth invested into real estate.

Notes

1. Evans et al. (2003), for example, explain how more autonomy goes hand in hand with homeownership.
2. Women are gaining importance in society; now representing the majority of graduate students, women account for around 60% of graduate and undergraduate students (Damisch et al. 2000).
3. Given that the first period budget is $A_1 = y_1 - c_1$ and the year before the last one is $A_{T-1} = y_{T-1} - c_{T-1} + (1 + r)A_{T-2}$; while the terminal budget is $0 = y_T - c_T + (1 + r)A_{T-1}$, multiplying each equation by $(1 + r)T - t$, we can sum up all budgets and all wealth levels simplify into the intertemporal budget constraint.
4. Using the Lagrangian function, the problem leads to the first order conditions, which show the optimal consumption evolution, stating the equality of consumption over time.
5. If uncertainty on lifetime length is considered in the framework, the conclusions of the model are not altered as transforming assets into annuities will neutralize life uncertainty (Yaari 1965).
6. Unemployment benefits can partially neutralize the risk of unemployment; however, they have a limited duration. Individuals are inevitably exposed to the risk of becoming unemployed as well as to income variations.

References

Alessie, R., & Lusardi, A. (1997). Consumption, saving and habit formation. *Economics Letters, 55*(1), 103–108.
Angelini, V., Laferrère, A., & Weber, G. (2013). Home-ownership in Europe: How did it happen? *Advances in Life Course Research, 18*(1), 83–90.
Becker, G. (1974). A theory of social interactions. *The Journal of Political Economy, 82*(6), 1063–1093.
Bricker, J., Kennickell, A. B., Moore, K. B., & Sabelhaus, J. (2012). Changes in U.S. family finances from 2007 to 2010: Evidence from the Survey of Consumer Finances. Federal Reserve Bulletin, Board of Governors of the Federal Reserve System (U.S.), issue June.
Brown, S., & Gray, D. (2016). Household finances and well-being in Australia: An empirical analysis of comparison effects. *Journal of Economic Psychology, 53*, 17–36.
Brown, S., & Taylor, K. B. (2016). Early influences on saving behaviour: Analysis of British panel data. *Journal of Banking and Finance, 62*, 1–14.
Chetty, R., Sándor, L., & Szeidl, A. (2017). The effect of housing on portfolio choice. *Journal of Finance, 72*(3), 1171–1212.
Coda Moscarola, F., Fornero, E., & Rossi, M. (2012). *Parents/children "deals": Inter-vivos transfers and living proximity*. CeRP WP N. 95/10. Retrieved from http://www.cerp.carloalberto.org/parentschildren-deals-inter-vivos-transfers-and-living-proximity-2/.
Damisch, P., Kumar, M., Zakrzewski, A., & Zhinlinskaya, N. (2000). Leveling the playing field: Upgrading the wealth management experience for women. The Boston Consulting Group, July 2010. Retrieved from http://www.bcg.com/documents/file 56704.pdf.
Deaton, A. (1992). *Understanding consumption*. Cambridge: Cambridge University Press.
Dietz, R. D., & Haurin, D. R. (2003). The social and private micro-level consequences of homeownership. *Journal of Urban Economics, 54*(3), 401–450.
Dynan, K. E. (2000). Habit formation in consumer preferences: Evidence from panel data. *American Economic Review, 90*, 391–406.
Evans, G. E., Wells, N. M., & Moch, A. (2003). Housing and mental health: A review of the evidence and a methodological and conceptual critique. *Journal of Social Issues, 59*, 475–500.

Friedman, M. (1957). *A theory of the consumption function*. Princeton: Princeton University Press.

Gambardella, D., Rossi, M. C., & Salomone, R. (2018). *Social finance as a public policy instrument*. CeRP WP 2018/178.

Guariglia, A. (2001). Saving behaviour and earnings uncertainty: Evidence from the British household panel survey. *Journal of Population Economics, 14*(4), 619634.

Guariglia, A., & Rossi, M. (2002). Habit formation and precautionary saving: Evidence from the British household panel survey. *Oxford Economic Papers, 54*, 1–19.

Kindermann, F., & Kohls, S. (2017). Rental Markets and wealth inequality across Europe. mimeo.

Kopczuk, W. (2015). What do we know about the evolution of top wealth shares in the United States? *Journal of Economic Perspectives, 29*(1), 47–66.

Marrella, P. (2014). *What now?: A widow's guide to financial independence.*

Mishra, A. K., Uematsu, H., & Powell, R. (2012). Precautionary wealth and income uncertainty: A household-level analysis. *Journal of Applied Economics, 15*(2), 353–369.

Modigliani, F., & Brumberg, R. (1954). Utility analysis and the consumption function. In *Post-Keynesian economics*.

Muellbauer, J. (2008). *Housing, Credit and Consumer Expenditure*. CEPR Discussion Papers 6782, C.E.P.R. Discussion Papers.

Piketty, T. (2014). *Capital in the 21st century*. Harvard: Harvard University Press.

Romiti, A., & Rossi, M. (2014). Housing wealth decumulation, portfolio composition and financial literacy among European elderly. Carlo Alberto Notebooks 375, Collegio Carlo Alberto.

Rossi, M. C. (2008). Households consumption under the habit formation hypothesis. Evidence from Italian households using the Survey of Household Income and Wealth (SHIW). In *Consumers Economics: New Research*. NOVA Publisher.

Rossi, M. (2009). Examining the interactions between savings and personal pension plan contributions. Evidence from the BHPS. *Oxford Bulletin of Economics and Statistics, 71*(2), 253–271.

Rossi, M. C., & Sansone, D. (2017). Precautionary savings and the self-employed, Netspar DP Accepted for publication in *Small Business Economics*.

Rossi, M. C., & Sierminska, E. (2015). *Single again? Saving patterns when widowhood occurs*. Luxembourg Institute of Socio-Economic Research (LISER) Working Paper Series, 2015–04.

Rossi, M., & Trucchi, S. (2016). Liquidity constraints and labor supply. *European Economic Review, 87*, 176–193.

Rossi, M. C., Sansone, D., van Soest, A., & Torricelli, C. (2018). *Household preferences for socially responsible investments*. Cefim WP 66. Retrieved from http://www.cefin.unimore.it/new/publications/household-preferences-for-socially-responsible-investments/.

Sherraden, M. (1991). *Assets and the poor: A new American welfare policy*. New York: M. E. Sharpe, Inc.

Sierminska, E. (2012). *Wealth in the crisis*. Social situation observatory: Income distribution and living conditions, Research note 09/2012, European Commission.

Yaari, M. (1965). Uncertain lifetime, life insurance and the theory of the consumer. *Review of Economics Studies, 32*, 137–150.

2

Wealth Variation Across Countries

Abstract In this chapter, we discuss the importance of wealth when considering the economic well-being of households and provide an overview of current wealth levels across countries in the EU and North America. We point to the relatively large variance of wealth levels within EU countries, including the UK (at the time of writing this chapter), as well as Canada and the US. In addition, we provide some suggestions of why there may be differences in wealth accumulation between women and men. We elaborate not only on the reasons for accumulation, which may differ, but also on the different ways women and men accumulate wealth. We discuss these differences in terms of wealth trajectories. In addition, we consider differences in wealth accumulation among families with and without children.

Keywords Wealth • Economic well-being • Families

We would like to thank Piotr Paradowski for helpful feedback.

© The Author(s) 2018
M. Rossi, E. M. Sierminska, *Wealth and Homeownership*,
https://doi.org/10.1007/978-3-319-92558-5_2

2.1 Why Wealth and Its Importance, a Gender Twist

Wealth, together with income and consumption, is considered to be an important determinant of economic well-being that is central in determining a household's economic security (Stiglitz et al. 2010). Economic well-being is primarily measured by financial means and is most often understood as a household's standard of living (OECD 2013). Somewhat surprisingly, wealth does not share the same long history as income when it comes to assessing its distribution and using it as a measure of the ability to make ends meet. And although wealth was discussed centuries ago only recently has there been a renewed interest in it in the literature. New advancements in data collection have made it possible to re-explore its role in economic well-being. It needs to be pointed out that wealth and income differ in an important way. Income is a flow variable, while wealth is a stock variable—as explained in Chap. 1 of this book. This stock variable can (and should) be annuitized at some point in the future, and, thus, it is a good measure of potential future income and consumption (Yaari 1965). In this way, it would be more accurate in assessing the potential (future) economic well-being than income. Total wealth is accumulated from savings and inheritance over time; thus, in the same way as total lifetime income, it can be considered as the best indicator, once normalized for the age and expected lifetime, of the welfare of an individual.

Wealth plays many roles. In addition to being an important component of economic well-being, it provides a buffer against shocks. In this role, it constitutes the first form of self-insurance. Non-negligible wealth amounts will protect households from the negative effects of financial adversities, such as irregular employment, by making them less vulnerable financially. The lack of wealth (or assets) requires people to live from one paycheck to the next. Having adequate wealth allows for consumption smoothing in times of financial strain and at other times for making larger purchases by loosening credit constraints. These could include acquiring vehicles, homes and education. An additional important role of wealth is that it provides collateral when credit is required. Thus, wealth can serve as a surety for credit and can be converted into cash to maintain consumption.

Wealth components may also contribute to income via interest and dividends (from financial assets such as stocks and mutual funds) and real estate in particular by providing a steady flow of rents. If needed, wealth can also be converted to cash, the speed of which depends on its liquidity.

Wealth in the form of real estate plays an additional role, as it generates current services such as accommodation. Owner-occupied housing, for example, provides services and frees up resources that would otherwise be spent on rent. Wealth and subsequently the value of your own home is also a determinant of residential location. Greater wealth will allow families to reside in areas with better schools and lower crime rates. It has an impact on school attendance, test scores and degree completion. Wealth enables families to provide better university education for their children. It is also associated with many outcomes that cannot be explained fully by income, such as educational attainment and health (Conley 2001).

Another important role of wealth (discussed below in more detail) is to provide a supplementary source of funding during retirement. This role of wealth is gaining in significance with the shrinking of the state provided pension system, a shift toward a lower replacement rate than in previous decades, and growing support for private pension saving plans. As elaborated later in this chapter, this is particularly important for women, who live longer than men and have lower pensions due to lower salaries and shorter working lives (Chang 2010).

Wealth can also serve as a source of power, including political power. It can also be passed on from generation to generation in the form of inheritance or transfers, thus encouraging wealth accumulation. The same situation would not take place for income as, in most cases, the right to income in the form of earnings is linked to a particular person.

As explained in the theoretical background in Chap. 1, when it comes to considering wealth with reference to the life cycle dimension, several life phases can be distinguished: the young, the middle aged, older households pre-retirement and older households post-retirement. Young households most often have low (close to zero or negative) wealth levels. For households, these coincide with a time in their life when they are finishing their education, possibly with outstanding loans, and are beginning their working careers. Over time, they will pay off their loans, save and begin the accumulation phase of their life (middle aged). The rate of accumulation will depend on various factors—including on the type of assets that are in the households' possession. Those with higher rates of return will allow for more intense accumulation and a steeper wealth profile. The accumulation process creates a stock of wealth that can be drawn upon during retirement. Households with individuals close to retirement age are expected to have wealth levels close to the maximum of their lifetime wealth. As individuals enter retirement, they begin decumulation and use some of their wealth in order to supplement their income and maintain their desired level of consumption. At some point during their life, inheritance may be passed on to them, increasing their stock of wealth. The cohort to which the individual belongs to is thus a crucial variable in determining the position in the wealth distribution and thus their economic status. Wealth, together with future incomes, determines the well-being of a household. For old households, where future incomes are less relevant (in contrast to young households), wealth could be a good proxy for well-being, that is, two households with similar levels of wealth will be considered equally well-off (as elaborated in Chap. 1, permanent income is the best measure of well-being).

2.1.1 A Gender Twist

The gender aspect does make a difference when it comes to wealth. As we will show in Sect. 2.2 and has been discussed at length in Sierminska (2017), the gender wealth gap is present and quite prominent. Here, we will discuss the sources of differences in wealth accumulation between women and men.

In most countries, women have higher life expectancy than men; thus, any accumulated wealth will need to sustain them for a longer time into the future. At the same time, women, on average, have shorter work experience and lower earnings. The lower attachment to the labor market results in lower accumulated wealth. Thus, women's lower wealth will need to last them for a longer time.

In addition, welfare states continue to shrink and the need to rely on private assets to ensure a comfortable retirement has increased; thus, the ability to accumulate wealth for retirement is more important than ever. Moreover, the share of single-person households has been steadily increasing. Nowadays, about half the households are headed by single persons and people are getting married later and later in life. As a result, women are spending more of their adult years single rather than married and have come to rely more and more on their own income and their own wealth. This makes it even more important for women to invest with maximum return in order to make ends meet and prepare properly for retirement. Obviously, no free lunch exists in the market; however, taking lower risk will turn, in the long run, into lower return, and this is usually the case for women's portfolios (Rossi and Sierminska 2015).

The literature on women around the age of retirement in North America shows the existence of a substantial gender wealth gap (Neelakantan and Chang 2010; Ruel and Hauser 2013 for the US; Denton and Boos 2007 for Canada). The situation in European countries may be considered as somewhat less severe, but there is substantial variation across countries. The largest wealth gap at the median is found in Austria, Germany and the Netherlands (0.42, 0.35 and 0.31, respectively) and the smallest in Luxembourg, Poland and Slovakia (0.90, 0.81 and 0.81, respectively) (data around the year 2011; Sierminska 2017). Older women typically have low levels of wealth, but their wealth holdings are generally higher than their country's median wealth holdings (Gornick et al. 2009).

Apart from the reasons mentioned above that contribute to the gender wealth gap, another factor that cannot be omitted from the discussion is the differential population aging and mortality rates between women and men. Women live longer; thus, if they become widows, an inheritance from their husband would have an equalizing effect on the wealth levels. Regarding this point, Deere and Doss (2006) highlight the importance of the marital and legal inheritance system for the well-being of women. In countries where the legal system derives from the Roman law, for example, Southern European countries, wives do not lose ownership of their personal property when they get married. This is due to the default marital regime system, which is partial community property.[1] This means that in the case of marriage dissolution, women retain their own individual property and receive half of the community property, as well.[2] Deere and

Doss (2006) argue that this system has been particularly favorable for wealth accumulation of married women in countries where this system prevails.

Another point to mention in the case of differing wealth levels is that women tend to marry older men who have had more time to accumulate wealth and who have higher education, a characteristic that is positively related to wealth accumulation (Gibson et al. 2006, for example). Thus, in full and partial community property regimes these women would fare well, but in those where separation of property regime exists (Anglo-Saxon countries) and divorce legislation does not guarantee an equal split of assets, women are more vulnerable.

Taking a closer look at the simple model of wealth accumulation will allow us to investigate in what respects the accumulation of women and men can differ. In the standard life cycle model, the stock of assets in the current period is the outcome of past decisions regarding investment, labor market behavior, (flow of) savings and consumption, and the stock of assets in the previous period. Thus, differences in any of these factors, or returns to these factors, for women and men (or any other groups) will give rise to a different accumulation pattern (Sierminska et al. 2010) and a different portfolio structure.

In the literature, it has been identified that women and men save differently; they have different access to wealth building tools; they invest differently with diverging levels of returns; and women have a weaker attachment to the labor market than men. Due to the economic crisis and changing work patterns, their roles have also evolved—particularly in the labor market. For example, the elderly in some countries support their children and grandchildren more than previously by relying on their accumulated wealth. These aspects are also gendered in nature.

Differences in investment attitudes can be seen via preferences for risk taking and realized portfolio decisions. Women are considered to be less risk-tolerant and more risk-averse (Cartwright 2011) than men. A difference in risk tolerance can be one of the factors that brings about differences in the portfolio of women and men and yields a different structure. Women's portfolios are typically less risky and have lower rates of return. However, this is being questioned more recently (Nelson 2015). In fact, Neelakantan and Chang (2010), using data for the US, show that the gender wealth gap is still present after controlling for risk preference differences between women and men. Financial literacy also influences investment decisions. Differences in financial knowledge among women and men yield more conservative investments being made by women (e.g. Lusardi and Mitchell 2008).

Apart from having differential returns from their investments, more risk-loving individuals (men) who have invested in risky assets will be more exposed to fluctuations in the (stock) market. Similarly, persons that invest the majority of their assets in real estate property will be very susceptible to changing house prices that will result in changing wealth levels.

It has also been argued that women make their asset allocation decisions differently because they are socialized differently and, consequently, different things are important to them. As a result, when it comes to investing, they focus on safer products (Chang 2010), excluding housing investment, on which we will focus in detail later on in this book.

When it comes to wealth building products, Chang (2010) identifies a *wealth escalator* that provides opportunities to build wealth and the *debt anchor* that causes wealth loss. This idea moves away from considering earnings as the main source of inequality between genders and points to something potentially equally or more important. With the same amount of income, the wealth escalator makes it possible to achieve higher levels of wealth in a shorter time through access to wealth building products. In the case of the US, this includes direct fringe benefits such as employer-sponsored retirement plans, traditional defined benefit plans and private pension savings. Since eligibility for these benefits is often governed by full-time employment,[3] women are more often not eligible for some of these benefits. In Europe, these deficiencies are reduced to some extent by the existing law that requires part-time workers to have access to benefits similar to those of full-time workers (based on the European Directive on Part-Time Work, 1997). Nevertheless, gender gaps in promotion, advancement opportunities and awarded bonuses within and across occupations disproportionally favoring men remain in Europe as well (Kauhanen 2017).

One of the most important (observable) factors that have been shown to explain male–female differences in wealth accumulation are labor market differences (Sierminska et al. 2010). These encompass a lower labor market participation rate of women, as well as fewer hours worked. Women more commonly work part-time (Bardasi and Gornick 2008; Matteazzi et al. 2014) compared to men who follow the standard pattern of continuous full-time employment. Women are also more likely to face interruptions in their working histories (Budig and England 2001; Gangl and Ziefle 2009) that further shorten the time spent in the labor market. Combine these factors with a long-standing gender pay gap and the choice of occupations and the result is a weaker position for women to accumulate wealth (Blau and Kahn 1997, 2000, 2016; Warren et al. 2001). Therefore, even if saving rates were held constant, we could expect women to accumulate lower levels of wealth in the future.

The recent crisis also had an additional gendered impact on wealth accumulation through the labor market. In several countries, the recession had a greater impact on male rather than on female employment (at least in the initial stage) and this translated into a decline of the gender wealth gap. In Spain and Germany, for example, the gender gap in wealth was becoming wider until the Great Recession and then it reversed (Sierminska 2017). The distribution of female employment worked to reduce female job losses (the segregation effect) since the first phase of the crisis mainly affected the male-dominated construction sector (Pena-Boquete 2014; Sierminska et al. 2008). As a result, male wealth accumulation decreased relative to that of females and the wealth gender gap began to narrow in the initial phase of the crisis.

2.1.2 Stylized Facts Regarding Wealth Accumulation Among Women and Men

In a recent report based on several country studies, Sierminska (2017) along with a group of experts identified several truths that can repeatedly be found across countries and, thus, consider these as stylized facts when it comes to wealth differences among women and men. For example, women on average (and at the median) have lower levels of wealth even though at the beginning of their adult lives they start with similar levels. There are no marked gender differences in inheritances received. Educational outcomes differ for women and men, and in recent years in some countries a larger share of women compared to men have completed higher education, but gender segregation in the field is still very present and is followed by earnings differences. These differences in personal characteristics contribute to the differences in wealth that emerge over the life course. In addition, the report finds that marital status affects men and women differently when it comes to wealth accumulation. Women focus more on saving products, while men on investment products and women participate less than men in investment tools. An important point is that women's portfolios are less risky. This could be the result of women being more risk-averse, and, since they earn less, could have the consequence that the expected rate of return on their portfolio is also lower. Bearing the foregoing points in mind, in the next section we review the latest evidence on the gender wealth gap in a subsample of EU countries.

2.2 Wealth Across Countries

Past literature has shown that we observe very different wealth levels across countries and that in many capitalist societies wealth levels tend to increase over time (Jäntti and Sierminska 2008; Kopczuk and Saez 2004; Kennickell 2009).

Wealth levels may differ across countries solely due to different institutional environments, which create incentives as well as disincentives for accumulating wealth. The institutional framework varies cross-nationally and, as such, it shapes the motivation and speed of wealth accumulation differentially. For example, it will influence private wealth needed at older ages. In some countries, greater emphasis is put on private wealth in order to finance retirement. In other countries, where welfare provisions are ensured by the government (such as Scandinavian countries) society does not feel the same pressure to accumulate wealth and thus lower wealth levels are present compared to those in countries with less generous pension systems. The structure of the education system is another example of institutions governing the demand for private wealth. In countries with high-quality public education, people will have lower incentives to save for kids' education compared to countries where the quality of private education is higher than that of public education.

Tax laws and the economic system also create incentives for wealth accumulation (Bover et al. 2016; Sierminska and Doorley 2013; Doorley and Sierminska 2014, study this extensively). A prominent example is that of the housing market and the associated mortgage market. A well-developed mortgage market will have an impact on the prevalence of homeownership. Countries that offer high loan to value (LTV) loans and interest deduction encourage mortgage take-up (Herbert et al. 2013). This can be particularly important for younger households and those liquidity constrained. In countries with lower capital gain taxes on financial products, financial investments will have more favorable conditions and may be encouraged (Guiso et al. 2002). It's good to keep in mind that the same institutions may either facilitate or limit wealth accumulation depending on the policies in place.

Wealth levels vary across countries according to the institutional environments. They also vary with the population structure. In younger societies, or in those where there are relatively younger less populated households, the average or median wealth levels tend to be smaller than in societies where we observe a larger prevalence of older (and larger) households (Bover 2010; Sierminska et al. 2013).

2.2.1 Wealth and Families

Country wealth varies with the population structure, while family structure is a strong indicator of wealth outcomes. It is a robust predictor of the number of earners in the family, their gender and their compensation. In the case of single-parent families, for example, there is one earner, usually a female that is commonly employed part-time. Family structure also determines access to tax and benefit programs and dictates economies of scale.[4]

Furthermore, the family type may impact the type of investments that are made and consequently will have a direct impact on asset accumulation. For example, married couples will be more likely to make joint investments compared to cohabiting couples with the same incomes. Joint investments are riskier for unmarried couples for whom the law is less clear on how to divide property in the event of separation and, thus, will be less common in not married households. Tax benefits are also linked to marital status such as is the case when it comes to housing investment. The entitlement to deduct mortgage interest and property taxes from taxable income is also linked to whether you are married or not and whether you are single-living alone or with other family members. In the US, the tax provisions for homeowners, the total amount paid in mortgage interest and property taxes must be higher than the standard deduction when filing taxes, which is twice as high for married couples than for individuals filing as single.

As will become evident in Chap. 3, family structure leads to differences in homeownership rates across family types. The main residence in a majority of countries is financed with the help of home mortgages; thus, differential homeownership across families will consequently lead to differences in mortgage debt. Heterogeneity is observed in this respect within family types, most commonly according to marital history, particularly for single parents and single-person households. Divorced singles (or single parents) are likely to have purchased a home while being married and subsequently depleted their savings and incurred debt due to divorce proceedings, which include high legal fees and setting up separate residences. Single-person households may also be more likely to accumulate credit card debt or other debts to smooth consumption in the event of unexpected earnings losses (e.g. due to unemployment or unpaid sick or maternity leave) and be more sensitive to income shocks compared to dual-earner families or even two-person single-earner families. Single—never married—parents are more likely to be renters and may be in a more precarious position than others, by never having the opportunity to accumulate enough savings to purchase their first home. Thus, homeownership and housing wealth may be the lowest among this group of parents.

Thus, the path according to which one becomes a single parent matters. Never married single parents by having had the least opportunity to accumulate joint wealth may be most vulnerable to economic hardship. Others that have a long marital history and are divorced, separated or widowed may be in a less precarious situation. Furthermore, the wealth situation will be very different for a person that became a parent at the age of 20 with little economic resources and a high school education versus a professional doctor with 15 years of work experience that went through divorce and received half of the joint assets. Of course, there exist innumerable variations in this respect, but the point remains that the trajectories of relationships for families plays a significant role in their accumulated wealth situation.

2.2.2 Median Wealth Levels

In what follows, we will show differences in wealth levels for a selected group of European and Anglo-Saxon countries. The choice of these countries is discussed in the methodological section that can be found at the end of this chapter (Sect. 2.5). In Fig. 2.1 (and Table 2.1), we find that median wealth levels vary a lot across countries worldwide. Not only are the differences quite striking across the globe, but we also find a lot of variation within Europe. We observe the highest median in Luxembourg (over 400,000 USD) and the lowest at 75,000 USD in Germany. The values for other European countries are within this range (Austria 105,000 USD, Finland and the Netherlands 125,000 USD, Greece 150,000 USD, France

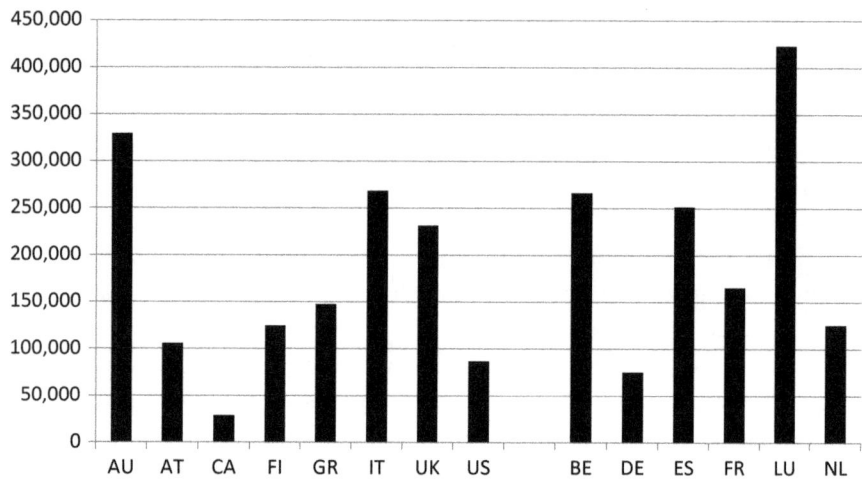

Fig. 2.1 Median net worth across selected countries (in 2011 USD). Source: Luxembourg Income Study (LIS) data (AU, AT, CA, FI, GR, IT, UK and US) and Household Finance and Consumption Survey (HFCS) (BE, DE, ES, FR, LU, NL). Note: *AU* Australia; *AT* Austria; *CA* Canada; *FI* Finland; *GR* Greece; *IT* Italy; *UK* United Kingdom and *US* United States; *BE* Belgium; *DE* Germany; *ES* Spain; *FR* France; *LU* Luxembourg; *NL* the Netherlands

Table 2.1 Median net worth and ratio over total by family types across selected countries (in 2011 USD)

	AU	AT	CA	FI	GR	IT	UK	US	BE	DE	ES	FR	LU	NL
Total	328,879	105,531	28,551	124,322	147,356	268,373	231,416	86,961	266,103	75,390	251,741	165,384	423,060	125,354
Single parents	218,086	25,004	–	48,876	79,216	133,253	131,599	45,080	129,333	27,954	192,442	58,808	196,916	60,759
Single with kids	127,561	43,658	–	46,673	102,921	238,503	55,103	13,328	162,849	11,927	209,748	14,040	318,048	39,812
Married parents	427,979	219,320	–	234,471	144,498	318,039	375,646	260,987	394,679	162,135	273,370	282,611	684,954	276,626
Married with kids	390,334	221,020	–	183,964	193,123	312,079	261,072	96,092	325,182	132,106	274,124	215,678	492,449	204,661
Ratio over total wealth														
Single	0.66	0.24	–	0.39	0.54	0.50	0.57	0.52	0.49	0.37	0.76	0.36	0.47	0.48
Single parents	0.39	0.41	–	0.38	0.70	0.89	0.24	0.15	0.61	0.16	0.83	0.08	0.75	0.32
Married	1.30	2.08	–	1.89	0.98	1.19	1.62	3.00	1.48	2.15	1.09	1.71	1.62	2.21
Married with kids	1.19	2.09	–	1.48	1.31	1.16	1.13	1.10	1.22	1.75	1.09	1.30	1.16	1.63
	AU	AT	CA	FI	GR	IT	UK	US	BE	DE	ES	FR	LU	NL
Total	328,879	105,531	28,551	124,322	147,356	268,373	231,416	86,961	266,103	75,390	251,741	165,384	423,060	125,354
Single female	249,908	25,721	–	61,117	86,113	132,132	185,833	50,155	210,333	23,854	199,730	92,955	225,839	39,067
Single male	188,244	23,632	–	39,218	46,348	143,215	92,875	39,200	59,505	33,297	160,973	38,689	170,020	69,040
Single mother	118,098	35,728	–	15,855	100,876	238,503	49,985	10,419	130,314	9890	200,658	11,187	312,364	35,879
Single father	184,334	146,830	–	133,939	141,908	243,466	144,150	27,873	227,115	153,190	265,426	78,920	1,077,434	93,614

(continued)

Table 2.1 (continued)

	AU	AT	CA	FI	GR	IT	UK	US	BE	DE	ES	FR	LU	NL
Ratio over total wealth														
Single female	0.76	0.24	–	0.49	0.58	0.49	0.80	0.58	0.79	0.32	0.79	0.56	0.53	0.31
Single male	0.57	0.22	–	0.32	0.31	0.53	0.40	0.45	0.22	0.44	0.64	0.23	0.40	0.55
Single mother	0.36	0.34	–	0.13	0.68	0.89	0.22	0.12	0.49	0.13	0.80	0.07	0.74	0.29
Single father	0.56	1.39	–	1.08	0.96	0.91	0.62	0.32	0.85	2.03	1.05	0.48	2.55	0.75

Source: LIS data (AU, AT, CA, FI, GR, IT, UK, US) and HFCS (BE, DE, ES, FR, LU, NL)
Note: AU Australia, AT Austria, CA Canada, FI Finland, GR Greece, IT Italy, UK United Kingdom, US United States, BE Belgium, DE Germany, ES Spain, FR France, LU Luxembourg, NL the Netherlands

165,000 USD, Spain 250,000 USD and Italy 270,000 USD). The remaining Anglo-Saxon countries, perhaps surprisingly, also exhibit very different levels of median wealth with the lowest levels in the US and the highest in Australia (US 86,000 USD, UK 230,000 USD and 330,000 USD).

The results above provide a general but mixed impression of median wealth levels across countries. In order to provide more details, in the subsequent table and figure (Table 2.1 and Fig. 2.2) we identify four main household types that are present throughout this book. These four types of households capture the majority of the population in each country and include single-person households, single parents, couples without children and couples with children. More details regarding the definition of these household types can be found in the methodological section at the end of this chapter (Sect. 2.5). In terms of wealth, these four household types follow different trajectories and are often at different phases in their life course. 1) Singles are most likely younger, never married or divorced individuals at the beginning of their accumulation stage or they are elderly—widowed households; 2) single parents are often women, possibly previously married. 3) Couples with or without children usually have the advantage of having more than one earner in the household; thus, the wealth accumulation process occurs at a higher pace for them and exceeds the expenses resulting from having a larger household. In our analysis, we focus on households that are headed by individuals between 26 and 75 years old. We exclude younger households as these may still be living at home or in dorms and attending university and we exclude older households as the existence of differential mortality rates across countries would begin to influence our results.

In Fig. 2.2 (and Table 2.1), we compare median wealth levels across countries for the different household types. First, we briefly compare wealth levels across family types and then we focus on within-country analysis. We see that in all countries couple households either with or without children have higher median wealth than either type of single-person households. When we zoom into the situation of households with only one adult, we find that in Anglo-Saxon countries single parents have lower median wealth than singles (Australia 128,000 USD vs. 218,000 USD, the UK 55,000 USD vs. 130,000 USD, and the US 45,000 USD vs. 87,000 USD). Countries such as Germany, France and the Netherlands also fall into this group. In Finland, these two types of families have more or less the same levels of wealth, while single parents are better off than

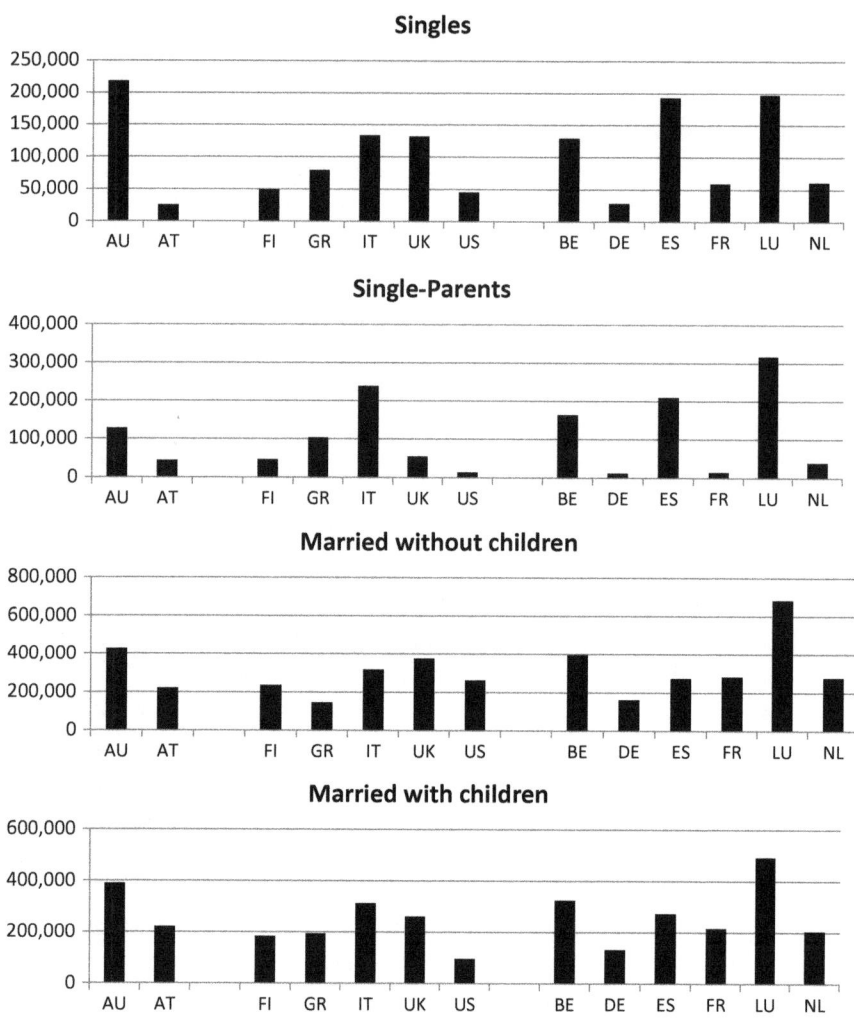

Fig. 2.2 Median net worth by family types across selected countries (in 2011 USD). Source: LIS data (AU, AT, CA, FI, GR, IT, UK and US) and HFCS (BE, DE, ES, FR, LU, NL). Note: *AU* Australia; *AT* Austria; *CA* Canada; *FI* Finland; *GR* Greece; *IT* Italy; *UK* United Kingdom and *US* United States; *BE* Belgium; *DE* Germany; *ES* Spain; *FR* France; *LU* Luxembourg; *NL* the Netherlands

singles in the remaining countries (Austria 44,000 USD vs. 25,000, Greece 103,000 USD vs. 80,000 USD, Italy 240,000 USD vs. 135,000 USD, Belgium 160,000 USD vs. 130,000 USD, Spain 210,000 USD vs. 192,000 USD, Luxembourg 320,000 USD vs. 197,000 USD).

Having seen that the situation of single-person households when it comes to wealth is substantially below that of the median household—we compare these differences across countries by calculating the ratio of their median wealth to that of the median household. In Table 2.1 we find that in most countries, single parents have less than half of the wealth at the hands of a median household. The worst situation is in France (0.08), the US (0.15), the UK (0.24) and the Netherlands (0.32). Single parents are best off in Italy (0.89), Spain (0.83), Luxembourg (0.75) and Greece (0.70).

Married couples and those with children (except in Greece) have higher levels of wealth than the median household in all countries, but here we also find different trends depending on the country.

2.2.3 Single-Female-Headed versus Male-Headed Households

The bottom panel in Table 2.1 also provides us with the distinction of single-person and single-parent households headed by a woman or a man. One-person households headed by women seem to be at a smaller disadvantage than those headed by men in most countries except in Italy, Germany and the Netherlands. Single-parent households, headed by men on the other hand, are better off than those headed by women. As mentioned previously, single households could be older households (widows) which have inherited wealth from their partner.

2.2.4 Age

In the previous Sect. 2.1, we outlined a life cycle perspective of wealth accumulation and pointed out factors that could explain differences in accumulation patterns across countries and family types. In the following figure (Figure 2.3), we attenuate this perspective by presenting results for different age groups and subsequently by family types (Figure 2.4).[5]

Figure 2.3 is an exposition of median wealth levels for different age groups. What is important to note here is that in all countries of our sample, median wealth levels are at their lowest for the youngest age group and then are systematically greater for older groups albeit at different rates. The

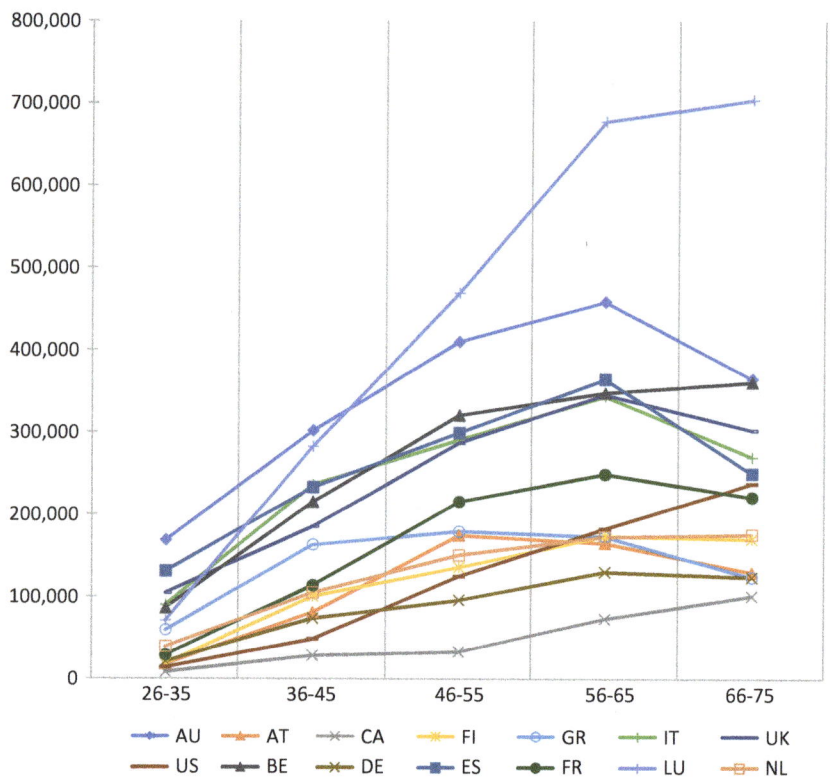

Fig. 2.3 Median net worth by age across selected countries (in 2011 USD). Source: LIS data (AU, AT, CA, FI, GR, IT, UK and US) and HFCS (BE, DE, ES, FR, LU, NL). Note: *AU* Australia; *AT* Austria; *CA* Canada; *FI* Finland; *GR* Greece; *IT* Italy; *UK* United Kingdom and *US* United States; *BE* Belgium; *DE* Germany; *ES* Spain; *FR* France; *LU* Luxembourg; *NL* the Netherlands

lowest wealth profile is for Canada, while the steepest is for Luxembourg and Australia. In almost all European countries, except Luxembourg,[6] the largest median wealth level is observed for the 56–65 age group.

2.2.5 Age and Family Type

The accumulation profile by age may be different for a married couple versus someone that is single. Thus, we compare differences in wealth levels by age and family type across countries. In Fig. 2.4, we find a bar

Wealth Variation Across Countries 37

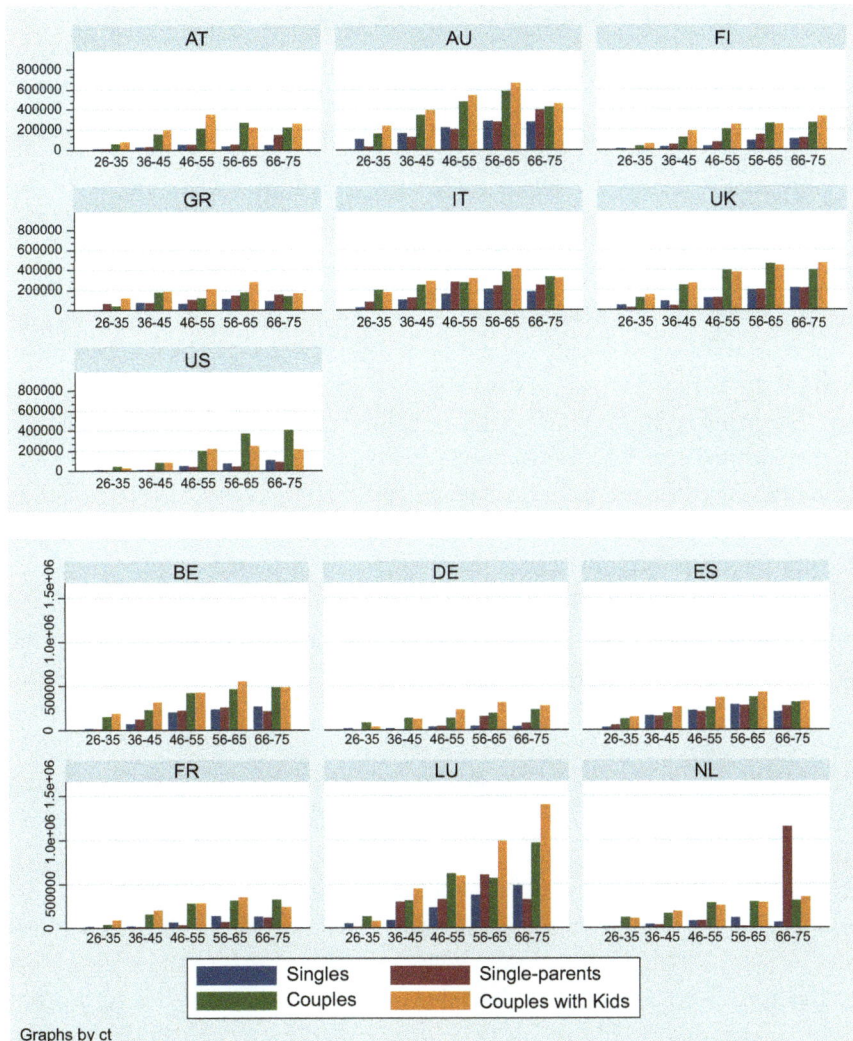

Fig. 2.4 Median net worth by age and family type across selected countries (in 2011 USD). Source: LIS data (AU, AT, CA, FI, GR, IT, UK and US) and HFCS (BE, DE, ES, FR, LU, NL). Note: *AU* Australia; *AT* Austria; *CA* Canada; *FI* Finland; *GR* Greece; *IT* Italy; *UK* United Kingdom and *US* United States; *BE* Belgium; *DE* Germany; *ES* Spain; *FR* France; *LU* Luxembourg; *NL* the Netherlands

graph representation of median wealth levels for different age groups and family types by country. As suspected, in all countries, couples have higher wealth levels than single-person households at all ages. Single-adult households start at a wealth disadvantage even in the youngest age group and this is accentuated among older age groups.

2.3 A Look into Housing as a Portfolio Component

Several cross-national studies have shown (Sierminska et al. 2006; Jäntti and Sierminska 2008; Sierminska 2017, an HFCS study) that one of the main components of a household wealth portfolio is housing. In many countries, the home comprises two-thirds of all assets or more. The cross-country differences in the share of real estate that are observed come from several factors. One of them is the prevalence of homeownership, which will be discussed in the following chapter. Here our interest lies in housing as a portfolio component. Home prices vary substantially cross-nationally (See Global Property Guide 2018). Home affordability varies as well. Sierminska et al. (2013) proxy affordability based on the relationship between gross housing values and income by focusing on home value-to-income ratios. By considering the mean as well as the median values they find that affordability defined in this way rises (home value-to-income ratio falls) as we move up the income distribution in all countries under consideration (Italy, Germany, Luxembourg, Sweden, the UK and the US) for the whole population, as well as single parents and couples with children. At the top of the income distribution, the ratios are in the range 8–10. Although conventional wisdom would suggest that homes are more affordable for couples with children than single parents, the results in their work show that this is not necessarily the case. The home value-to-income ratios are lower for single parents in Germany and Sweden than in other countries.

In what follows, we compare the importance of housing in the portfolio across different countries in our sample.

In Table 2.2 you will find the average value of the principal residence, as well as that of total assets and home equity, which is the value less the

Table 2.2 Average value of principal residence, total assets and home equity across selected countries (in 2011 USD)

	AU	AT	CA	FI	GR	IT	UK	US	BE	DE	ES	FR	LU	NL
Principal residence	270,830	143,214	85,032	182,903	128,668	217,674	237,554	202,081	244,924	119,370	240,974	159,005	452,801	185,210
Total assets	541,265	307,475	157,207	234,684	229,817	379,710	435,556	579,163	473,201	304,181	452,172	331,238	880,489	297,213
Home equity	222,183	127,365	61,312	140,239	115,693	205,586	186,815	123,305	210,966	95,852	211,395	142,301	387,674	110,826
As a share of total assets														
Principal residence	50	47	54	78	56	57	55	35	52	39	53	48	51	62
Home equity	41	41	39	60	50	54	43	21	45	32	47	43	44	37
Percent of homes owned without a mortgage	82	89	72	77	90	94	79	61	86	80	88	89	86	60

Source: LIS data (AU, AT, CA, FI, GR, IT, UK, US) and HFCS (BE, DE, ES, FR, LU, NL)
Note: AU Australia, AT Austria, CA Canada, FI Finland, GR Greece, IT Italy, UK United Kingdom, US United States, BE Belgium, DE Germany, ES Spain, FR France, LU Luxembourg, NL the Netherlands

mortgage taken out on the property. Home values exhibit great dispersion. The lowest home values are found in Canada (85,000 USD), followed by those in the 100,000 USD range: Germany, Greece, Austria, France, Finland, the Netherlands; and then those in the 200,000 USD range: the US, Italy, the UK, Spain, Belgium, Australia. The most expensive homes in this group of countries are in Luxembourg (450,000 USD). To examine the share of assets held in real estate, our interest here lies in two values. The first is the ratio of the gross housing value and total assets, which is the potential wealth a household could imagine having in housing if there are no loans to consider. This varies from a low share of about 35–40% in the US and Germany to about 50% in Australia, Austria, Belgium, Spain, France, Luxembourg and about 55% in Canada, Greece, Italy and the UK. The two highest shares are in the Netherlands (62%) and in Finland (78%). This also provides an indication of the liquidity of the portfolio. The higher the share of housing in the portfolio, the less liquid it is.

The second value is home equity as a share of total assets. This value, as defined in the previous paragraph, takes into account any loans that need to be paid off (having used the house as collateral) if we were to liquidate the principal residence. This ratio varies from a low 21% in the US (32% in Germany; 37% in the Netherlands; 39% in Canada; 41–45% in Australia, Austria, Belgium, Spain, France, Luxembourg and the UK; and 50% in Greece and 54% in Italy) to a high 60% in Finland. There are at least two factors that contribute to this dispersion in ratios. The first are country variations in housing prices and the second the country-specific ability to take out loans by households, which depends on the economic institutions in the country and whether the households are liquidity constrained.

The final row indicates what is the percentage of homes owned outright (without any mortgage) on average. The lowest value is to be found in the Netherlands and the US at 60% and the highest at above 90% in Greece and Italy. The in-between values at about 75% are in Canada and Finland; and at 80% in Australia, Austria, Belgium, Germany, Spain, France and Luxembourg.

2.3.1 Families

Table 2.2 shows the population average indicators for real estate; we also provide these details by family type in order to better understand which type of families are more liquid when it comes to their household wealth portfolio and which ones are liquidity constrained. In Table 2.3 we have three panels: Panel 1 shows the ratios of the value of the principal residence and total assets, panel 2 that of home equity and total assets and panel 3 the percentage of principal residence owned outright, without a mortgage.

In Table 2.3, we find that, systematically, in almost all countries families that are married and without children are most liquid, since they exhibit the lowest share of housing as a percent of total assets among the other family types. Greece and Italy are the exceptions. The highest ratio

Table 2.3 Principal residence and home equity as a share of total assets and percent of principal residence owned outright across countries (in 2011 USD)

	AU	AT	FI	GR	IT	UK	US	BE	DE	ES	FR	LU	NL
Principal residence													
Single	55	47	77	63	61	56	41	53	34	59	47	55	60
Single parent	57	70	80	66	71	55	57	54	49	62	56	79	62
Married	47	45	77	60	57	51	30	49	38	52	46	45	61
Married + kids	50	46	79	53	55	57	36	53	43	51	49	50	65
Home equity													
Single	48	44	60	60	58	48	27	48	29	54	44	44	35
Single parent	45	65	56	59	67	41	28	46	38	56	47	73	34
Married	42	41	67	56	56	45	21	46	32	48	44	42	43
Married + kids	38	39	53	46	51	39	19	41	32	44	41	41	35
% Owned													
Single	87	94	78	95	94	85	65	91	84	92	92	80	59
Single parent	79	92	70	89	95	75	48	86	78	90	84	93	54
Married	88	91	87	94	97	89	71	93	85	91	96	93	70
Married + kids	76	84	67	87	93	68	53	78	74	85	83	81	54

Source: LIS data (AU, AT, CA, FI, GR, IT, UK and US) and HFCS (BE, DE, ES, FR, LU, NL)

Note: *AU* Australia; *AT* Austria; *CA* Canada; *FI* Finland; *GR* Greece; *IT* Italy; *UK* the United Kingdom and *US* the United States; *BE* Belgium; *DE* Germany; *ES* Spain; *FR* France; *LU* Luxembourg; *NL* the Netherlands is usually for single parents (Panel 1). Married couples with children exhibit the lowest percent of outright ownership, except in the US, where single parents are the ones with the lowest share of outright ownership.

2.3.2 Consequences of Homeownership

The decision to purchase a home is one of the most difficult decisions a family will consider during their lifetime (also one of the more stressful ones). Entering homeownership will bring about several consequences for individuals and families and the literature suggests that there are arguments both for and against homeownership (for an overview, see Herbert et al. 2013). In addition to economic rationale, in some countries, being a homeowner is considered a value per se and owning a home is viewed as a sign of economic achievement.[7] Moreover, as discussed below, several governmental policies have been directed toward enhancing homeownership.[8]

Changes in wealth are cited as the most important consequence of homeownership (Dietz and Haurin 2003) and several studies have proven that a strong correlation exists between homeownership and wealth levels in the US, as well as in EU countries (Bricker et al. 2012; Sierminska 2012) to such an extent that homeownership is considered to be a good predictor of total wealth. Although, on average, the majority of people own their own home, the decision to become a homeowner differs strongly across the wealth distribution (Bertaut and Starr-McCluer 2002). In the lower quartile of the wealth distribution in the US, there are very few homeowners. Homeownership increases as one moves toward the median of the distribution, with real estate becoming a major asset for the middle class. As we move up the wealth distribution, a more balanced portfolio is increasingly present with financial assets gaining a more prominent role in the portfolio.

While for the majority of people, the capital tied up in their primary (and, most of the time, only) residence constitutes their entire wealth, at the macro level, housing is also important, as in most countries over 50% of wealth is tied up in housing and thus the overall economy is also very sensitive to developments in the housing market (Mathä et al. 2014).

Housing decisions are a difficult subject to examine as housing in itself contains several components: housing is an investment, insurance and a commodity providing housing services, as illustrated in Chap. 1. Homeownership thus provides a household with a composite good. First of all, a flow of housing services has to be accommodated, as a household needs a place to reside. Second, ownership is also an investment in real estate, which exposes households to price fluctuations. Given that a house is both an investment good and a consumption good it could be that homeowners have more investment risk than renters. At the same time, it constitutes a hedge against rental risk.

To become a homeowner, a consistent effort is required, which could displace other (more lucrative) investments or force households to reduce consumption at early stages of the life cycle. Thus, homeownership could also be costly in terms of foregone alternative investments, particularly if housing equity becomes a larger and larger multiple of income over time. This happens with increasing housing price levels and decreasing outstanding loan principals.

Homeownership could also be discouraging financial risk taking by homeowners. At the same time, homeowners can also help boost the economy as they consume from their home's capital gains[9] via home equity loans and can rely on housing to provide security in times of income fluctuations. In most cases, from a portfolio balance perspective, investment in housing is greater than optimal with even older households holding a majority of their wealth in housing (Gornick et al. 2009; Fisher et al. 2007).

From a policy standpoint, it is reassuring to observe that a majority of households own their house, thus implying that in a case of income fluctuation they have an asset to rely upon and consequently could be at a lower risk of poverty.

2.3.3 Families

For a family, getting on the homeownership ladder represents a crucial step in their savings decisions, as we will discuss in more detail in Chap. 4. Housing is seen as a vehicle to accumulate assets as it fosters an orientation toward the future (Sherraden 1991), that can result in a higher rate of wealth accumulation than in the case of renting. By buying a house, households start the accumulation process and protect themselves against rent price fluctuations. Owning a house can represent security against economic vulnerability. For a family, homeownership is an important way to accumulate wealth through forced saving, in the form of monthly mortgage payments and through a possible appreciation in value. Housing tenure implies that by paying off their mortgage, households accumulate housing equity, which can function as a financial reserve. Money invested in housing is further extended through tax benefits aimed specifically at homeowners. Homeowners in the US, for example, are allowed to deduct mortgage interest and property tax deductions on their primary and secondary residences.[10] Homeownership creates benefits at different ages. Apart from serving as a financial reserve, owning a home and paying off the mortgage allows an individual to save for retirement and to gain financially due to long-term home price appreciation. In fact, the mere act of assuming mortgage debt may also induce a long-term commitment to the household by prompting a change in household spending behavior and thus "forcing" the household to save by paying down the mortgage. In this way, households pre-commit to a scheme, which is costly to break. Over recent decades, however, the effectiveness of using one's house as a means of forced savings has weakened considerably, given the increased prominence of housing equity withdrawal and mortgage refinancing, particularly in the US (Li and Yang 2010).

Homeownership can also be seen as an economic decision that presents the advantage of reducing the risk of increased costs associated with rental prices (Sinai and Souleles 2005; Calcagno and Rossi 2011). At the same time, households become more vulnerable to price fluctuations of the future sale. Moreover, while the rental risk is neutralized, a consistent part of wealth is tied up in an illiquid asset, which could prove an obstacle in smoothing consumption over time if it becomes difficult to get access to immediate liquidity. Brunetti et al. (2015) with reference to Italian households suggest that homeownership is another marker of financial fragility due to its relative lower liquidity. The cost of owning could be a burden to families that are faced with income fluctuations (e.g. unexpected job loss) as paying off the mortgage could be a major expense and, given that it is an illiquid asset, it could be very costly for homeowners to adjust in response to an economic shock. In this case, illiquidity of real estate could force households to drastically reduce their standard of living in the case of employment loss or a health issue. In that sense, homeownership can represent a form of financial distress that is not necessarily related to (over) indebtedness. A decrease in housing prices can be another form of risk for people who buy a house with a mortgage, causing some families to go under water, with a negative net housing value (Horsewood and Neuteboom 2006).

When it comes to specific family types, for single parents and for low-income households in general, homeownership may cause particular difficulties. Research has found that low-income households have more difficulty in maintaining ownership status. They have less ability to deduct mortgage interest and property taxes from taxable income. When taking a mortgage, there are systematic differences in terms and conditions, depending on income, that also may affect the financial return. There is a wider variation in mortgage terms and pricing than ever before and an extensive literature documents an increase in subprime lending to minorities and, though to a lesser extent, to low-income borrowers and communities (e.g. Do and Paley 2013; Finke et al. 2005). In addition, low-income homebuyers may be more likely to purchase homes in poor conditions and are therefore exposed to greater risks of high maintenance and repair costs. They may also be more likely to purchase homes in neighborhoods with less potential for house price increases. Evidence shows that there is discrimination on the basis of gender and marital status when it comes to lending in the housing markets (Ladd 1998). This may result in different rates of homeownership and different levels of home equity, with lower rates of homeownership and lower home equity for single-mother households and unmarried couples, *ceteris paribus*. It is important to note that for single parents homeownership may also become burdensome as they solely provide the maintenance on the home without the support of a partner, which may become a substantial liability for those with limited income and significant home expenses.

In the end, whether owning a home will lead to an accumulation of wealth will depend on a complex set of factors, related both to the choices that households make in buying their home and to how these choices interact with market conditions at the time of the purchase as well as over time. In addition, there may be substantial selection effects on homeownership as there is reason to believe that those who are in a more secure position and thereby are more inclined to save money are also more likely to become homeowners.

2.4 Methodological Issues in Measuring Wealth

2.4.1 What Is Wealth?

Wealth comprises many components including assets that can be easily liquefied and those more illiquid. Alternatively, it consists of financial and non-financial assets. Non-financial assets is one of the main components of the wealth portfolio. These consist of real estate, in particular the households' principal residence—the focus of this book; other real estate properties; and vehicles, consumer goods and valuables. Apart from non-financial assets wealth also refers to financial assets such as current accounts, savings accounts and other investment tools (mutual funds, bonds, publicly traded shares, managed investment accounts, private pensions and others). Financial assets exclude public and occupational pension plans as well.

2.4.2 The Challenge of Cross-National Wealth Comparisons

Cross-country comparisons are very often filled with challenges. A common challenge is the lack of cross-country comparable data. This may be the result of data collection efforts, where only information for a selected set of components is collected or it may be that a specific investment tool does not exist in all countries under consideration and thus, information on this tool is collected for a subset of countries. Discerning the two requires quite detailed country-specific and institutional knowledge. Another possibility would be to access a database that has already undertaken this effort and provides harmonized wealth data, which means that values across different countries are comparable as much as possible. To this end, we make use of the most recent waves of the Luxembourg Wealth Study (LWS) Database and supplement it with data from the Euro area countries, the HFCS, when the country data that includes wealth is not present in the LWS database (See Appendix of this chapter for details on the data).

2.5 Summary

In this chapter, we highlighted the differences that exist in wealth across countries and outlined some of the factors that could be contributing to these differences.

In particular a comparison was done to highlight the differing access to wealth among the population overall and for various family types that can be representative of women and men (overall, couples without kids, couples with kids, singles [women or men] without kids, single parents [women or men]). We also targeted populations at different stages in their life cycle. We pointed out that widespread differences exist by family type and by gender. We also zoom in with the life cycle perspective in mind and present information for different age groups.

Appendix: Data, Variables and Family Types

Data

The data in this chapter comes from two large data sets. The first comes from the LIS Cross-National Data Center (LIS 2016) from the latest wave of the LWS Database. The LWS provides cross-nationally harmonized microdata on both income and wealth for several high-income countries. Apart from income and wealth information, it also contains demographic variables at the household and individual level. We chose countries with the most recent data, which represent various welfare systems and correspond as much as possible to the countries available for our study on homeownership in Chap. 3. These include Australia, Austria, Canada, Finland, Greece, Italy, the UK and the US.

In order to enlarge our list of European countries, we also made use of the first wave of the Euro System HFCS data. This data set contains information on wealth, income and sociodemographic characteristics of over 62,000 households from 15 countries of the Euro area collected between 2010 and 2011.[11] Here we included Belgium, Germany, Spain, France, Luxembourg and the Netherlands to correspond as much as possible to the countries selected in Chap. 3.

Variables

In this chapter, we use the wealth variables that include total net worth, total assets, the value of real estate and in particular the value of the principal residence, as well as real estate liabilities. In addition, we use several demographic variables at the household level that allowed us to define several household types such as household composition, number of children, marital status.

We top code wealth at the 99th percentile and bottom code at the 1st percentile. The monetary values are converted to 2011 US dollar using the 2011 consumer price indices (CPIs) and 2011 USD PPP published on the LIS website. All our statistics are weighted with the use of appropriate weights.

An important aspect of the wealth data is that it is collected at the household level. Thus, in couple households, the person that answers the survey is classified as the head of the household. In most cases, this person is considered to be "the most financially knowledgeable person in the household."

Family Types

For the purpose of this study, we define four household types. They are defined as follows: (1) single one-person household; (2) single-parent household (one adult and at least one child under 18 years of age); (3) couples without children (two adults married or cohabiting); (4) couples with children (two adults and at least one child under 18 years of age).

In Canada, the data provider does not include variables that would allow us to define specific household types. Nevertheless, the case for Canada is extremely interesting; thus we include this country in our analysis at the more aggregate level.

Notes

1. This regime creates community property of any earnings, as well as other assets acquired by the couple during the marriage.
2. In Austria, for example, most married couples share their real estate wealth equally (Wagner 2012). In couples with unequal ownership, men are more likely to be the ones owning a greater share. Interestingly, a much greater share of single women bought their main residences (62% of women vs. 12% of men, and 53% of married couples), while single men were much more likely to have inherited their main residences (41% of men and 12% of women). The opposite was the case for other type of real estate: single men were more likely to have purchased investment property, while single women were twice as likely to have inherited their investment real estate.
3. Even this varies by employer and sectors in the economy.
4. The discussion in the section on wealth and families draws on Sierminska (2018).
5. It should be noted that we do not follow cohorts over time and are instead presenting differences in wealth levels for different age groups for a given year.
6. Luxembourg is somewhat of an exception, being one of the wealthiest countries in the world and having a large population of European civil servants; similar is the case for Belgium. For a first analysis of gender wealth differences in this country see Weber and Sierminska (2017) and for Belgium see Kuypers and Marx (2014).
7. A 2010 US Department of Commerce Report listed homeownership as one of the aspirations of the middle class. Values and goals can be strong determinants driving the purchase of a house (see Coolen et al. 2002).
8. To this end, in the US, for example, the American Dream Down Payment Assistance Act was introduced in 2003 as a temporary program aimed at helping low-income households become homeowners. In this country, owning a home is a well-known aspiration of the middle class and in the

words of some authors "the American dream has become an American obsession" (Li and Yang 2010).
9. Federal Reserve Chairman Alan Greenspan argued this helped to soften the 2001 recession in the wake of a drop in the value of other assets.
10. In many EU countries, like in the US, policies are in place that promote homeownership at a large scale, including low- and middle-income classes.
11. HFCS fieldwork took place in 2010/2011 for most of the countries. Exceptions include France (data collected in 2009/2010), Greece (data collected in 2009) and Spain (data collected in 2008/2009).

References

Bardasi, E., & Gornick, J. (2008). Working for less? Women's part-time wage penalties across countries. *Feminist Economics, 14*(1), 37–72.

Bertaut, C. C., & Starr-McCluer, M. (2002). Household portfolios in the United States. In L. Guiso, M. Haliassor, & T. Jappelli (Eds.), *Household portfolios*. The MIT Press.

Blau, F. D., & Kahn, L. M. (1997). Swimming upstream: Trends in the gender wage differential in the 1980s. *Journal of Labor Economics, 15*, 1–42.

Blau, F. D., & Kahn, L. M. (2000). Gender differences in pay. *Journal of Economic Perspectives, 14*, 75–99.

Blau, F. D., & Kahn, L. M. (2016). *The gender wage gap: Extent, trends, and explanations*. NBER Working Paper No. 21913.

Bover, O. (2010). Wealth inequality and household structure: U.S. vs. Spain. *Review of Income and Wealth, International Association for Research in Income and Wealth, 56*(2), 259–290.

Bover, O., Casado, J. M., Consta, S., Du Caju, P., McCarthy, Y., Sierminska, E., et al. (2016). The distribution of debt across Euro-area countries: The role of individual characteristics, institutions and credit conditions. *International Journal of Central Banking, 12*(2), 71–128.

Bricker, J., Kennickell, A. B., & Moore, K. B. (2012). Changes in U. S. family finances from 2007 to 2010: Evidence from the survey of consumer finances. *Federal Reserve Bulletin, 98*(2), 1–80.

Brunetti, M., Giarda, E., & Torricelli, C. (2015). Is financial fragility a matter of illiquidity? An appraisal for Italian households. *Review of Income and Wealth*, on-line March, 2015. https://doi.org/10.1111/roiw.12189.

Budig, M. J., & England, P. (2001). The wage penalty for motherhood. *American Sociological Review, 66*, 204–225.

Calcagno, R., & Rossi, M. (2011). Portfolio choice and precautionary savings. *Economics Bulletin, 31*(2), 1353–1361.

Cartwright, E. (2011). *Behavioral economics*. New York: Routledge.

Chang, M. L. (2010). *Shortchanged: Why women have less wealth and what can be done about it*. New York: Oxford University Press.

Conley, D. (2001). Capital for college: Parental assets and postsecondary schooling. *Sociology of Education, 74*(1), 59–72.

Coolen, H., Boelhouwer, P., & van Driel, K. (2002). Values and goals as determinants of intended tenure choice. *Journal of Housing and the Built Environment, 17*(3), 215–236.

Deere, C. D., & Doss, C. R. (2006). The gender asset gap: What do we know and why does it matter? *Feminist Economics, 12*(1–2), 1–50.

Denton, M., & Boos, L. (2007). The gender wealth gap: Structural and material constraints and implications for later life. *Journal of Women & Aging, 19*(3–4), 105–120.

Dietz, R. D., & Haurin, D. R. (2003). The social and private micro-level consequences of homeownership. *Journal of Urban Economics, 54*(3), 401–450.

Do, C., & Paley, I. (2013). Does gender affect mortgage choice? Evidence from the US. *Feminist Economics, 19*(2), 33–68.

Doorley, K., & Sierminska, E. (2014). Cross-national differences in wealth portfolios at the intensive margin: Is there a role for policy? *Research on Economic Inequality, 22*, 43–85.

Finke, M., Huston, S., Siman, E., & Corlija, M. (2005). Characteristics of recent adjustable-rate mortgage borrowers. *Financial Counseling and Planning, 16*(2), 17–28.

Fisher, J., Johnson, D., Marchand, J. T., Smeeding, T. M., & Boyle Torrey, B. (2007). No place like home: Older adults, housing, and the life-cycle. *Journal of Gerontology Social Science, 62B*(2), 8120–8128.

Gangl, M., & Ziefle, A. (2009). Motherhood, labor force behavior, and women's careers: An empirical assessment of the wage penalty for motherhood in Britain, Germany, and the United States. *Demography, 46*(2), 341–369.

Gibson, J., Le, T., & Scobie, G. (2006). Household bargaining over wealth and the adequacy of women's retirement incomes in New Zealand. *Feminist Economics, 12*(1–2), 221–246.

Global Property Guide. (2018). Retrieved from http://www.globalpropertyguide.com/Europe/square-meter-prices.

Gornick, J. C., Sierminska, E., & Smeeding, T. M. (2009). The income and wealth packages of older women in cross-national perspective. *Journal of Gerontology: Social Sciences, 64B*(3), 402–414.

Guiso, L., Haliassos, M., & Jappelli, T. (2002). *Household portfolios*. Cambridge: MIT Press.

Herbert C. E., McCue, D. T., & Sanchez-Moyano, R. (2013). *Is homeownership still an effecting means of building wealth for low-income and minority households? (Was it ever?)*. Joint Center for Housing Studies, Harvard University.

Horsewood, N., & Neuteboom, P., editors (2006). The Social Limits to Growth: Security and Insecurity Aspects of Home Ownership, Delft University Press, December.

Jäntti, M., & Sierminska, E. (2008). Survey estimates of wealth holdings in OECD countries: Evidence on the level and distribution across selected countries. In J. B. Davies (Ed.), *Personal wealth from a global perspective*, Chapter 2. UNU-WIDER Studies in Development Economics, Oxford University Press.

Kauhanen, A. (2017). Gender differences in corporate hierarchies. *IZA World of Labor, 358*. https://doi.org/10.15185/izawol.358.

Kennickell, A. B. (2009–2013). *Ponds and streams: Wealth and income in the U.S., 1989 to 2007*. Finance and Economics Discussion Series.

Kopczuk, W., & Saez, E. (2004). Top wealth shares in the United States, 1916–2000: Evidence from estate tax returns. *National Tax Journal, National Tax Association, 57*(2), 445–487. Retrieved from https://ideas.repec.org/a/ntj/journl/v57y2004i2p445-87.html.

Kuypers, S., & Marx, I. (2014), De verdeling van de vermogens in België [The distribution of wealth in Belgium], CSB Bericht No.1, Antwerp: Herman Deleeck Centre for Social Policy, University of Antwerp.

Ladd, H. F. (1998). Evidence on discrimination in credit markets. *Journal of Economic Perspectives, 1*, 223–234.

Li, W., & Yang, F. (2010). American dream or American obsession? The economic benefits and costs of homeownership. *Federal Reserve Bank of Philadelphia Business Review*, 20–30. Retrieved from http://www.phil.frb.org/econ/br/index.html.

LIS. (2016). *Luxembourg wealth study database (LWS)*. Luxembourg: LIS. Retrieved July, 2016, from www.lisdatacenter.org.

Lusardi, A., & Mitchell, O. S. (2008). Planning and financial literacy: How do women fare? *American Economic Review: Papers & Proceedings, 98*(2), 413–417.

Mathä, T., Porpiglia, A., Ziegelmeyer, M. (2014, May). *Wealth differences across borders and the effect of real estate price dynamics: Evidence from two household surveys*. ECB Working Paper Series No. 1672.

Matteazzi, E., Pailhe, A., & Solaz, A. (2014). Part-time wage penalties for women in prime age. *ILR Review, Cornell University, ILR School, 67*(3), 955–985.

Neelakantan, U., & Chang, Y. (2010). Gender differences in wealth at retirement. *American Economic Review, 100*(2), 362–367.

Nelson, J. A. (2015). Are women really more risk-averse than men? *Journal of Economic Surveys, 29*(3), 566–585. https://doi.org/10.1111/joes.12069.

OECD. (2013). *OECD framework for statistics on the distribution of household income, consumption and wealth*. Paris: OECD Publishing.

Pena-Boquete, Y. (2014). Have the economic crises reduced the gender gap on the Spanish labour market? *Revue de l'OFCE, 133*(2), 277–302.

Rossi, C., & Sierminska, E. (2015). Single again? Saving patterns when widowhood occurs. *LISER Working Paper Series 2015–04*, LISER.

Ruel, E., & Hauser, R. M. (2013). Explaining the gender wealth gap. *Demography, 50*(4), 1155–1176.

Sherraden, M. (1991). *Assets and the poor: A new American welfare policy*. New York: M. E. Sharpe, Inc.

Sierminska, E. (2012). *Wealth in the crisis, Social situation observatory: Income distribution and living conditions*. Research note 09/2012, European Commission. December.

Sierminska, E. (2017). *Wealth and gender in Europe, vol. 1 Main report*. Report for the European Commission, Directorate General: Justice and Consumers.

Sierminska, E. (2018). The 'wealth-being' of single parents. In L. Maldonado & R. Nieuwenhuis (Eds.), *The triple bind of single-parent families*, Chapter 13. Policy Press.

Sierminska, E., & Doorley, K. (2013). *To Own or Not to Own? Household Portfolios, Demographics and Institutions in a Cross-National Perspective* (IZA Discussion Papers 7734). Bonn: Institute for the Study of Labor (IZA).

Sierminska, E., Brandolini, A., & Smeeding, T. M. (2006). The Luxembourg wealth study—A cross-country database for household wealth research. *Journal of Economic Inequality, 4*(3), 375–383.

Sierminska, E. M., Frick, J. R., & Grabka, M. M. (2010). Examining the gender wealth gap. *Oxford Economic Papers, 62*(4), 669–690.

Sierminska, E., Smeeding, T. M., & Allegrezza, S. (2013). The distribution of assets and debt. In J. Gornick & M. Jäntti (Eds.), *Income inequality: Economic disparities and the middle class in affluent countries* (pp. 285–311). Stanford, CA: Stanford University Press.

Sierminska, E., Piazzalunga, D., & Grabka, M. (2018). *Transitioning towards more equality?: Wealth gender differences and the changing role of explanatory factors over time*. Unpublished manuscript.

Sinai, T., & Souleles, N. S. (2005). Owner-occupied housing as a hedge against rent risk. *The Quarterly Journal of Economics, 120*(2), 763–789.

Stiglitz, J. E., Sen, A., & Fitoussi, J.-P. (2010). *Report by the commission on the measurement of economic performance and social progress.* Retrieved January 12, from http://graphics8.nytimes.com/packages/pdf/business/Stiglitzreport.pdf.

Wagner, K. (2012). Wie ist das Immobilienvermögen zwischen Verheirateten aufgeteilt? Statistiken – Daten & Analysen, Q3/12, 71–89

Warren, T., Rowlingson, K., & Whyley, C. (2001). Female finances: Gender wage gaps and gender assets gaps. *Work, Employment and Society, 15*, 465–488.

Yaari, M. (1965). Uncertain lifetime, life insurance and the theory of the consumer. *Review of Economics Studies, 32*, 137–150.

3

Families and Housing Decisions: A Look Across OECD Countries

Abstract Homeownership trends developed in 22 OECD countries over the past three to four decades are examined and differences related to the homeownership gap for women and men are discussed, with a focus on most recent trends. The US and countries with varying institutional structures are compared with particular attention being paid to differences across family types. The estimation techniques allow us to discuss the role of determinants from a gender perspective. We find that single women are better off than single men without children and a reverse trend exists in families with children. The general negative effect for women remains for younger cohorts in the face of risking homeownership. The latest crisis did not change the general long-running trend of the homeownership gap except for the US and France. The findings of this chapter provide an international perspective on differential homeownership rates among women and men, across countries and over time. Given that the value of one's own home (home equity) is the largest financial reserve in a household's wealth portfolio, it is important to have a better understanding of the differences resulting from gender and family types.

Keywords Housing • Families • Cross-National Comparisons • United States

3.1 Introduction

Having discussed the role of wealth and of housing wealth in a household's portfolio in the previous chapter, in this chapter we turn toward the decision of owning your own home—potentially one of the most important decisions during a person's life. In the first part of the chapter, we examine homeownership trends that have developed in 22 OECD countries over the last three to four decades and compare the differential trends across countries, while making regional distinctions.

Next, we propose to look into homeownership according to differences in household structures and the gender of the household's head. Given that homeownership represents the first pillar of wealth, housing wealth can be of paramount importance particularly as a buffer stock after retirement, despite being an illiquid asset, and hence less easy to be fungible. With a smaller welfare state, households might need to resort to withdrawing funds from their real estate (e.g. see Dillingh et al. 2017). For these reasons, it is important to understand the population's homeownership structure to detect whether there are any possibly vulnerable groups among families. Do these ownership patterns differ across countries?

Thus, in the next section of the chapter, we measure whether there exists a homeownership gap between women and men or rather by family type. We pay particular attention to the most recent trends. We compare the existing differences in the US to those in countries with different institutional structures and in particular with respect to differences across family types.

Subsequently, in the last part of the chapter, we move away from raw differences that exist across countries and focus on estimation techniques that allow us to discuss the role of determinants from a gender and family perspective.

The results point to a clear pattern that emerges when it comes to household types and homeownership rates. Single women are better off than single men without children. In families with children, a reverse trend emerges. The general negative effect for women remains for younger cohorts in the face of risking homeownership. The latest crisis did not change the general long-running trend of the homeownership gap except for the US and France. Our findings provide an international perspective on differential homeownership rates among women and men, across countries and over time. Given that the value of one's own home (home equity) is the largest financial reserve in a household's wealth portfolio, we argue that it is important to have a better understanding of the differences resulting from gender and family types.

3.2 Motivation

Homeownership decisions represent a critical step in household asset management and may even be the most important decision in life for a majority of households (Chambers et al. 2003). Entering into homeownership is a crucial decision taken at the family level and is one of the most important commitments (both financially and in other respects) during the life cycle. If the home is not purchased outright, paying mortgage installments absorbs a major part of a family's monthly income.

Over the past decades, OECD countries have witnessed an increasing trend in homeownership, which brought about several changes not only for families, but also at the more aggregate level of the economy. At the micro level—the focus here—homeownership is not only seen as a vehicle for wealth accumulation, as discussed in detail in Chap. 2, but it is also positively correlated with several other outcomes. It contributes to the economic health of communities as people who are homeowners are invested in their communities and work on enhancing their neighborhoods. In addition, homeowners are on average better performers (economically speaking) than non-homeowners; thus, encouraging homeownership may contribute to increasing the economic well-being of households. Moreover, the educational and future prospects for children residing in owned houses show better results (Haurin et al. 2002). However, owning your own home also reduces mobility and thus potentially could reduce job search opportunities and thus increase unemployment (Oswald 1996). Evidence indicates that homeowners are less likely to be unemployed, but have lower wages, most likely due to the need to hold a job in a reasonable proximity to their owned home and in order to make their monthly payments.

Particularly among women, substantial changes have been observed in the housing market over the past decade. Women have been shown to be purchasing homes at a very high rate (McGinn 2013). There could be several reasons for this. On the one hand, homeownership provides women with financial security and reduces their fear of being homeless. On the other hand, a lower stigma in the housing market than in the financial market has encouraged women in their 20s to buy condos and even second residence homes as purchasing a home is seen as a less risky investment than investing money in the stock market. As housing contains an investment component as well as a consumption component, women could be more inclined to invest in the housing market by being more distant from the financial market in general. Potentially, concentrating their wealth in a less liquid asset such as housing could make them more vulnerable and may lead to a suboptimal ownership plan. But, at the same time, women could also be more inclined to invest in the housing market, because they are more risk-averse than men and by focusing on the housing market they are protecting themselves from the more volatile financial market. Single households may also be more likely in a suboptimal ownership pattern since they have greater difficulty in buying dwellings. Thus, the type of household to which a person belongs could potentially be one of the most relevant factors determining homeownership and not gender *per se*. We explore this in this chapter.

3.3 Data and Methods

In our focus on homeownership rates, we use data from the Luxembourg Income Study (LIS) Cross-National Data Center (www.lisdatacenter.org) from the 1970s, 1980s, 1990s and the first decade of the twenty-first century. The use of this data archive offers many advantages as it provides cross-nationally harmonized income and wealth microdata across many different countries and over time. The LIS database that is used here contains harmonized microdata from a large number of mostly high-income countries. It contains information on market income, public transfers and taxes, household and personal characteristics, and labor market outcomes. In total, data for over 40 countries is available from the 1970s, but the time dimension is not available for all countries. Our criteria for selecting countries for the study were to have several years of data, information on homeownership and some basic demographic variables. We also wanted countries to represent several geographical areas; thus in the end we are able to include a set of countries for Northern Europe (Denmark, Finland, Ireland, the Netherlands, Sweden and the UK), Central Europe (Austria, Belgium, France, Germany, Luxembourg and Switzerland), Eastern Europe (Estonia, Poland and Russia), Southern Europe (Greece, Italy and Spain), North America (Canada, the US and Mexico) and Israel. A list of countries along with their respective years can be found in the Chapter Appendix (Table 3.5).

An important aspect of the LIS data is that it is collected at the household level. Thus, in couple households the gender of the household is classified as the one of the respondent of the survey. In most cases, this is the most financially knowledgeable person in the household.

3.4 Empirical Analysis

In our analysis, we first examine homeownership rates over time to capture the different trends that exist across countries and then observe the raw gaps between women and men homeowners.

Next, we estimate a pooled probit on homeownership across countries to check whether the homeownership gaps are specific to women and men or perhaps family types. We distinguish several family types: single (one-person households), single with kids (single person with children under 18), married (two-person households), married with kids (two-person households with children), cohabiting (two-person households), cohabiting with children (two-person household with children) and other multi-person households. We also control for age, age squared, university degree, whether the person is employed or unemployed, log of household disposable income and tenure (years worked at current job) and the wave the data is coming from. We also include several interactions with the female indicator (0/1). The list of variables used in the analysis along with their labels can be found in the Appendix (Table 3.6). The list of countries chosen for the analysis along with the names of the original surveys can be found in the Appendix (Table 3.7).

3.5 Descriptive Statistics

As per the latest wave of data available at LIS at the time of writing this chapter, homeownership rates (in Table 3.1) show remarkable differences across countries. Around the year 2010, the highest rates are present in ex-Soviet countries (more than 80% in Estonia, Poland and Russia), possibly due to the transition policy of allowing households to become owners of the occupied residence. Among non-ex-communist countries, the modal highest rate is around 70%, with the peak at 82% in Spain. It seems feasible for there to be a natural rate of non-ownership (or natural rate of absence of homeownership—NAHO). The statistics indicate that around 10–15% of households are not homeowners, which in fact is compatible with the demographic structure of the population, where young families still need to build up a buffer before becoming homeowners. In addition, young households are required to be more mobile, for which being tied to one's home can become an impediment.

3.6 Homeownership Across Time

Looking at the homeownership trend over time as summarized in Table 3.1, we can see variation across countries. Striking evidence of increasing homeownership rates over time can be observed in about half of the countries (e.g. in the Netherlands, Poland, Canada and the US), while it has remained stable or even diminished in others (e.g. Finland, Ireland, Italy, Mexico and Israel).

The variation in changes during the 1990–2000 decade is not very pronounced: the change varies from less than −4 ppt to about 5 ppt. The Netherlands (8.9 ppt increase), Poland (8.3 ppt increase) and Sweden (11.8 ppt decline) are the only exceptions to this rule. In the second period from 2000 to 2010, which encompasses the Great Recession, financial crisis in the US and Europe and mild recovery (stagnation), the change is more pronounced with a wider variation from an 8 ppt drop to a 4 ppt increase with the exception of Ireland (14 ppt drop) and Poland (14.9 ppt increase). Some countries—Finland, the UK, Mexico and Israel—have witnessed a feeble decline of below 6 ppt in homeownership over the last 20 years

(1990–2010). In other countries, such as Ireland, Luxembourg and Greece, the decline is more pronounced (over 10 ppt), which could be attributed to an unusually high homeownership rate to begin with or the recent increase in housing prices, which makes it difficult for the young to get on the ownership ladder. A modest increase in homeownership took place in Germany, Italy and Canada (less than 5 ppt) and virtually no change occurred in the US. A substantial increase in homeownership rates took place in Poland. In the post-communist countries, the homeownership rate is over 80%, which is unusually high compared to the other countries. This is most likely due

Table 3.1 Homeownership rates and changes over time

Waves	1980s	1990s	2000s	Pre-crisis	Post-crisis/2010	Change 1990–2000	Change 2000–2010	Change 1990–2010
	1	2	3	4	5			
Northern Europe								
Denmark		58.5	63.0			4.5		
Finland	75.5	73.0	69.7	70.9	71.8	−3.3	2.1	−1.2
Ireland		83.4	85.9	77.4	71.9	2.4	−14.0	−11.6
Netherlands		51.2	60.1	62.2	62.7	8.9	2.6	11.5
Sweden	42.5	55.1	43.3			−11.8		
UK	60.3	70.6	72.6	72.2	68.3	2.0	−4.2	−2.3
Central Europe								
Austria	45.9	54.1	54.3			0.2		
Belgium	65.3	68.8	74.1			5.3		
France	55.3	58.4	58.2			−0.2		
Germany	44.8	42.1	42.9	44.3	46.8	0.8	3.9	4.7
Luxembourg	67.1	72.9	70.2	70.2	62.7	−2.7	−7.5	−10.2
Switzerland		39.6	38.8			−0.8		
Eastern Europe								
Estonia			86.8	87.8	82.3		−4.6	
Poland		58.4	66.8	80.9	81.7	8.3	14.9	23.2
Russia			92.2	91.8	92.5		0.3	
Southern Europe								
Italy		65.8	68.2	69.5	68.1	2.4	−0.1	2.3
Spain			84.5	82.5	82.0		−2.5	
Greece		83.6	79.9	74.0	72.2	−3.7	−7.7	−11.4
North America and Israel								
Canada	67.4	67.2	71.6	71.5	70.8	4.4	−0.9	3.6
Mexico		79.5	75.8	74.3	73.7	−3.6	−2.1	−5.8
US	67.4	67.8	71.3	70.4	68.2	3.5	−3.1	0.4
Israel		76.0	73.4	71.2	71.1	−2.6	−2.3	−4.8

Source: LIS data; own calculations

to the favorable privatization policies that took place after the fall of communism at which time cooperative housing was massively privatized. In Western Europe, the country that registered the highest increase of ownership rate is the Netherlands at 11 ppts.[1]

3.7 Gender Dimension, Family Structure and Homeownership

Next, we re-examine the changing homeownership rates with respect to gender. Looking at the gender dimension in Fig. 3.1, stable evidence emerges. In the countries under consideration, women have a lower homeownership rate than men, but the gap in homeownership is not stable over time and varies a lot across countries. What is striking is that the difference in homeownership persists in many countries. The general homeownership trend when decomposed into that of women and men is not always easily spotted in the homeownership pattern of both genders separately.

The trend points to a rise in women's homeownership rates over the past decades (Fig. 3.1) and a decrease of the gender gap in most countries. Perhaps this is due to a more recent decline in homeownership after the Great Recession. The gap is very small in countries such as Austria, Luxembourg, Finland, Italy and Spain. The gap has increased in a handful of countries such as Belgium, the Netherlands and Switzerland.

Household structure has changed rapidly over the last century and thus the observed gender differences may in fact be driven by differences in family types. Moreover, previous literature states that demographics will exert a powerful influence on future housing demand (Belsky 2009). Single households have become more common in most countries and families change more rapidly than in the past due to the increasing rate of divorce and remarriage. We show these more detailed trends of the evolution of family types in the Appendix (Table 3.8).

A more detailed analysis of homeownership thus calls for examining the trends taking into consideration family types. These results, broken down by gender, can be found in Fig. 3.2 and the Appendix (Fig. 3.5).

Families and Housing Decisions: A Look Across OECD Countries

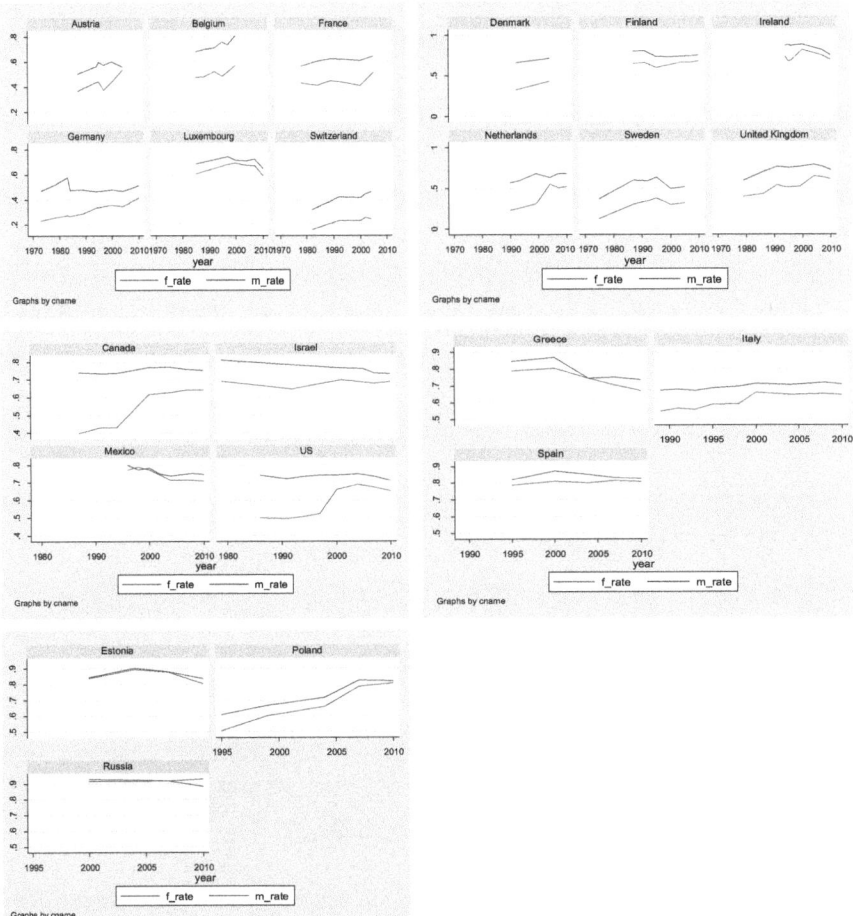

Fig. 3.1 Homeownership rates by country for women and men household heads. Source: LIS data; own calculations

Our goal in what follows is to first detect if there is a common characteristic among similar family types across countries and in the following section to see if these findings hold when controlling for other factors. The focus in this section is on six household types (described previously in the data section): single and married with or without kids, headed by a female or a male.

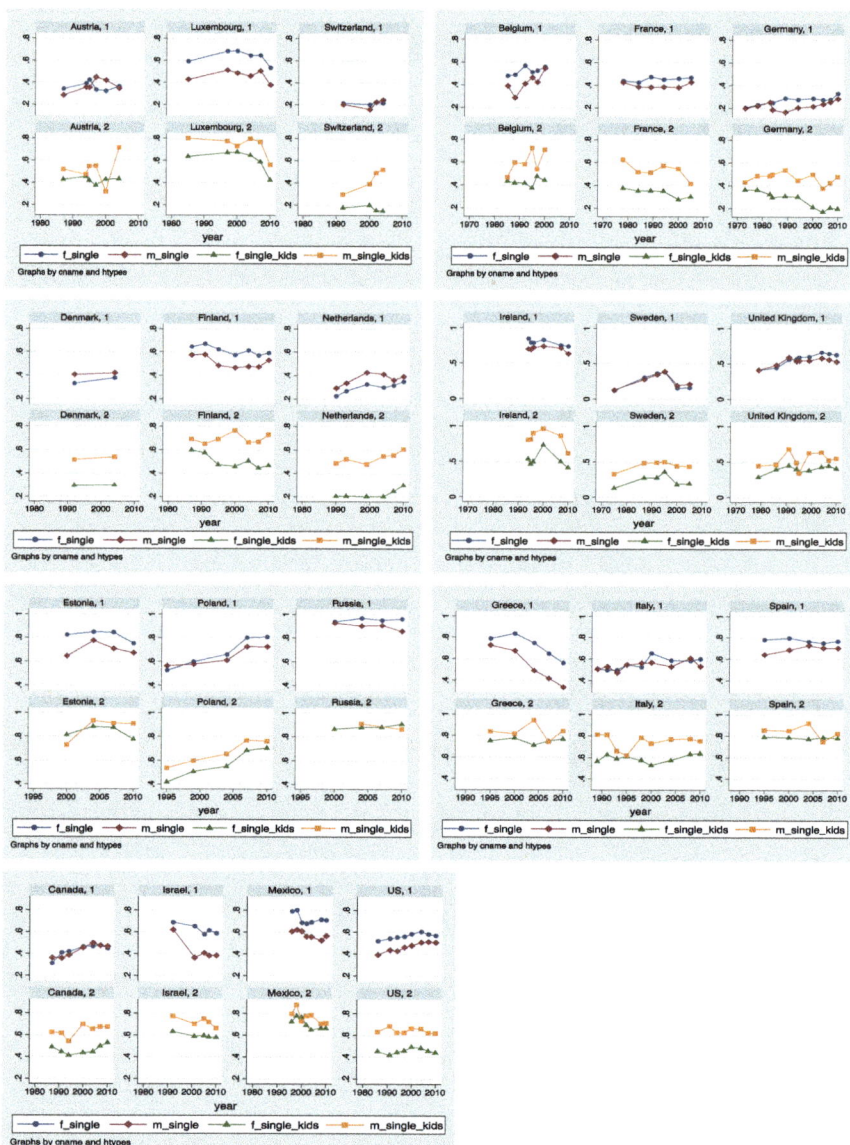

Fig. 3.2 Homeownership rates by family type across decades (for singles and singles with kids). Source: LIS data; own elaboration

It should be noted that for a married couple, it is difficult to distinguish the role of gender. In fact, the household head's gender is typically male, which leaves us with very few observations for female-headed households. In addition, in many countries focusing on the household head tells us little about the actual homeownership, as there is a 50–50% split of assets and most often the decision to own a home is made jointly by a couple.[2] Nevertheless, we show this distinction in the Appendix (Fig. 3.5) in order to show the general trend of ownership over time among couples and in order to compare the differences for couples with and without children. The pattern of homeownership for married couples shows an increasing trend whether these families have children or not. No clear pattern emerges irrespective of whether those with or without children have higher levels of ownership. A more meaningful and clear-cut approach to examining gender differences in homeownership is to focus on households with one adult only.

Single households by definition have one adult member who has to decide about her/his ownership patterns. A general emerging pattern shown in Fig. 3.2 is that single women are more likely to be homeowners. This reveals that, in fact, among singles, in most countries men are in the more vulnerable category. The exceptions seem to be Switzerland, Sweden, Italy and Canada where the homeownership gap is very small or non-existent. Single men are much more likely to be homeowners than women in Denmark and the Netherlands and this is unusual compared to other countries, where no gap or a gap in favor of women is oberved. Once children are involved, the trend reverses, and in most countries, there is a significant homeownership gap in favor of male-headed single households with children. Thus, another finding resulting from the descriptive evidence is that having children seems to act as a homeownership enhancer for men, but not for women. Homeownership rates for single mothers are considerably lower than for single women without children.

3.8 Estimation Results

In the following section, we estimate several probit regressions on the pooled sample of waves for several countries. We have chosen the countries for which it was possible to collect basic information on the determinants of owning a house, such as marital status, number of children, living arrangement, age of the head of the household, education level, employment status, tenure at work and income level. The goal of this analysis is to determine whether using the multivariate analysis confirms that single women are still more oriented toward homeownership or if the effect vanishes once income levels and other characteristics are controlled for. We estimate these models for the whole sample, and for singles only, separately for two cohorts: those 25–45 and those 46–65 years old.

3.8.1 Whole Sample

Our results first concern the whole sample. Table 3.2 shows that the effect of being a female tout court is in most cases negative and significant. In eight countries (out of 14), being female has a statistically significant negative effect on homeownership. The most negative effect of being a woman is seen in Luxembourg and Austria, where the probability of homeownership for women is lower by 39 and 36 ppt, respectively. The only country where the effect is positive and statistically significant is Denmark. In this country, controlling for other factors, women have an increased chance of being homeowners by 25 ppts. In the Netherlands, Germany, France, Spain and Greece, the female indicator is not significant. We cannot, thus, conclude that women have a diverse preference structure for housing than men, as it, nevertheless, varies across countries. Family type, on the other hand, has a clearer impact on ownership. Single status, in all countries, is a deterrent to homeownership as being single is associated with a lower probability of owning a house. This evidence could be attributed to the absence of economies of scale, which makes getting on the property ladder easier if the purchase is made as a couple. Single women, though, have higher possibilities than men to be homeowners, except in Denmark. Thus, the descriptive evidence of single women being more likely than men to be owners found in the previous graphs does not vanish when other controls are allowed. With the exception of Denmark, where single women are worse off than single men, in all other countries they are more likely to invest in housing than

Table 3.2 Homeownership probit estimates for the pooled sample of waves (marginal effects)

	Finland (1)	Denmark (2)	Netherlands (3)	UK (4)	Germany (5)	France (6)	Austria (7)
Female (d)	−0.059*	0.250***	−0.090	−0.103***	0.051	−0.008	−0.359***
	(−1.72)	(8.45)	(−1.45)	(−3.69)	(1.35)	(−0.20)	(−8.61)
Single (d)	−0.446***	−0.097***	−0.171***	−0.093***	−0.370***	−0.294***	−0.428***
	(−29.15)	(−9.51)	(−5.95)	(−10.49)	(−36.37)	(−24.58)	(−33.38)
Single*female	0.103***	−0.062***	0.137***	0.093***	0.101***	0.126***	0.151***
	(10.16)	(−4.15)	(4.49)	(7.96)	(4.38)	(6.64)	(7.67)
Single + kids	−0.328***	−0.038**	−0.086**	−0.094***	−0.163***	−0.198***	−0.325***
	(−11.94)	(−2.31)	(−2.20)	(−6.21)	(−7.00)	(−8.94)	(−10.99)
(Single + kids)*female	0.026	−0.180***	−0.002	−0.021	−0.051	0.007	0.125***
	(1.30)	(−9.22)	(−0.03)	(−1.16)	(−1.56)	(0.25)	(3.98)
Married (d)	−0.154***	0.220***	0.087***	0.140***	−0.164***	−0.026**	−0.307***
	(−12.03)	(22.75)	(3.76)	(20.50)	(−14.01)	(−2.25)	(−24.51)
Married*female	0.078***	−0.277***	0.175***	0.018	0.125***	0.155***	0.181***
	(6.40)	(−20.06)	(7.16)	(1.19)	(5.35)	(6.77)	(8.17)
Married + kids	−0.086***	0.278***	0.168***	0.136***	−0.008	0.027**	−0.135***
	(−8.45)	(30.99)	(7.42)	(19.59)	(−0.65)	(2.53)	(−11.15)
(Married + kids)*female	0.077***	−0.068***	0.207***	−0.020	0.158***	0.172***	0.219***
	(6.37)	(−4.38)	(9.62)	(−1.23)	(7.10)	(8.56)	(12.30)
Cohabiting	−0.316***	0.025**	0.013	0.053***	−0.301***	−0.253***	−0.408***
	(−17.53)	(2.23)	(0.49)	(5.53)	(−23.54)	(−16.62)	(−23.84)
Cohabiting*female	0.081***	0.100***	0.171***	−0.001	0.185***	0.134***	0.192***
	(6.51)	(5.36)	(6.62)	(−0.07)	(6.61)	(4.50)	(4.01)
Cohabiting + kids	−0.226***	0.145***	0.111***	0.018	−0.247***	−0.159***	−0.331***
	(−12.71)	(13.74)	(4.94)	(1.60)	(−13.00)	(−11.00)	(−15.63)
(Cohabiting + kids)*female	0.090***	0.072***	0.142***	−0.061***	0.156***	0.169***	0.251***
	(7.43)	(3.56)	(4.53)	(−2.61)	(4.61)	(6.73)	(7.52)

(continued)

Table 3.2 (continued)

	Finland (1)	Denmark (2)	Netherlands (3)	UK (4)	Germany (5)	France (6)	Austria (7)
Age	0.020***	0.013***	0.020***	0.012***	0.020***	0.043***	0.031***
	(21.01)	(14.54)	(12.37)	(15.03)	(15.66)	(33.34)	(20.36)
Age2	−0.000***	−0.000***	−0.000***	−0.000***	−0.000***	−0.000***	−0.000***
	(−12.82)	(−6.21)	(−10.25)	(−6.24)	(−8.02)	(−23.24)	(−15.47)
University degree	0.047***	0.071***	0.146***	0.131***	0.064***	0.090***	0.007
	(14.82)	(22.81)	(29.76)	(32.93)	(13.17)	(17.52)	(0.73)
Unemployed	−0.105***	0.061***	−0.068***	−0.090***	−0.147***	−0.182***	−0.260***
	(−9.10)	(5.96)	(−2.77)	(−9.25)	(−12.09)	(−13.33)	(−11.60)
Unemployed*female	−0.003	0.047***	0.016	0.046***	0.024	0.022	0.096***
	(−0.20)	(2.90)	(0.46)	(3.18)	(1.14)	(1.05)	(2.97)
Employed (d)	0.103***	0.276***	0.158***	0.252***	0.085***	0.030***	0.001
	(17.18)	(73.67)	(19.12)	(56.09)	(12.75)	(3.88)	(0.09)
Log income	0.020***	0.060***	−0.002	0.000	0.005**	0.039***	−0.093***
	(11.95)	(31.38)	(−0.67)	(0.13)	(2.22)	(16.55)	(−29.89)
Log income*female	−0.008***	−0.026***	−0.014**	0.004	−0.020***	−0.016***	0.019***
	(−2.62)	(−9.73)	(−2.57)	(1.36)	(−5.65)	(−3.59)	(4.25)
Tenure	0.004***		0.004***	0.005***	0.005***		0.007***
	(7.63)		(4.81)	(20.00)	(16.35)		(3.98)
Tenure*female	−0.001*		0.001	0.005***	−0.003***		−0.007**
	(−1.82)		(0.33)	(9.39)	(−5.05)		(−2.26)
N	63,134	142,238	38,145	125,282	83,014	67,267	40,820

(continued)

Table 3.2 (continued)

	Luxembourg (8)	Belgium (9)	Italy (10)	Spain (11)	Greece (12)	US (13)	Canada (14)
Female (d)	−0.392***	−0.246**	−0.138***	−0.012	−0.055	−0.066***	−0.167***
	(−5.08)	(−2.23)	(−3.34)	(−0.38)	(−1.09)	(−4.36)	(−6.24)
Single (d)	−0.314***	−0.251***	−0.250***	−0.110***	−0.292***	−0.215***	−0.237***
	(−12.09)	(−6.95)	(−20.46)	(−9.53)	(−14.38)	(−56.46)	(−33.87)
Single*female	0.174***	0.119***	0.073***	0.055***	0.080***	0.075***	0.031***
	(7.06)	(3.02)	(4.78)	(5.30)	(4.79)	(18.17)	(3.88)
Single + kids	−0.159***	−0.129**	−0.155***	−0.049**	−0.139***	−0.031***	−0.114***
	(−3.20)	(−2.39)	(−6.68)	(−2.16)	(−2.81)	(−5.15)	(−10.08)
(Single + kids)*female	0.078*	0.022	0.021	0.026	0.024	−0.059***	−0.022*
	(1.73)	(0.36)	(0.86)	(1.33)	(0.62)	(−8.01)	(−1.82)
Married (d)	−0.060**	0.019	−0.089***	0.030***	−0.108***	0.122***	0.051***
	(−2.44)	(0.68)	(−8.84)	(4.02)	(−7.46)	(43.02)	(10.23)
Married*female	0.085**	0.065	0.079***	0.032**	0.071***	0.053***	0.058***
	(2.48)	(0.71)	(4.55)	(2.49)	(3.71)	(10.42)	(6.56)
Married + kids	−0.013	0.110***	−0.064***	0.046***	−0.096***	0.170***	0.136***
	(−0.60)	(4.21)	(−7.57)	(6.82)	(−8.80)	(64.10)	(30.30)
(Married + kids)*female	0.112***	0.030	0.092***	0.040***	0.077***	0.072***	0.026***
	(3.84)	(0.40)	(6.43)	(3.89)	(4.96)	(17.36)	(2.76)
Cohabiting	−0.198***	−0.182***	−0.248***	−0.049***	−0.364***	−0.079***	−0.082***
	(−5.90)	(−4.09)	(−7.39)	(−2.83)	(−6.32)	(−9.48)	(−8.13)
Cohabiting*female	0.144***	0.148***	−0.003	0.051***	0.063	0.056***	0.061***
	(4.30)	(3.31)	(−0.06)	(2.78)	(1.24)	(5.64)	(5.10)
Cohabiting + kids	−0.189***	−0.083*	−0.242***	−0.066***	−0.153*	−0.026***	0.026***
	(−5.58)	(−1.96)	(−5.70)	(−3.43)	(−1.88)	(−3.17)	(3.26)
(Cohabiting + kids)*female	0.167***	0.080	−0.020	0.072***	0.098*	0.041***	0.048***
	(5.81)	(1.17)	(−0.31)	(4.41)	(1.83)	(3.93)	(3.67)

(continued)

Table 3.2 (continued)

	Luxembourg (8)	Belgium (9)	Italy (10)	Spain (11)	Greece (12)	US (13)	Canada (14)
Age	0.005**	0.032***	0.029***	0.015***	0.022***	0.027***	0.020***
	(2.11)	(13.19)	(22.15)	(12.88)	(12.87)	(64.96)	(27.13)
Age2	0.000	−0.000***	−0.000***	−0.000***	−0.000***	−0.000***	−0.000***
	(0.83)	(−9.12)	(−15.98)	(−8.21)	(−7.92)	(−36.47)	(−15.41)
University degree	0.037***	0.055***	0.107***	0.033***	−0.000	0.107***	0.055***
	(4.45)	(6.26)	(17.92)	(8.24)	(−0.05)	(72.98)	(21.50)
Unemployed	−0.376***	−0.108***	−0.183***	−0.090***	−0.130***	−0.042***	−0.041***
	(−11.13)	(−3.76)	(−12.34)	(−7.18)	(−5.98)	(−8.03)	(−5.68)
Unemployed*female	0.067*	−0.001	0.077***	−0.002	0.072***	−0.017**	0.011
	(1.77)	(−0.02)	(3.51)	(−0.15)	(4.15)	(−2.29)	(0.94)
Employed (d)	−0.108***	0.108***	−0.019***	0.011*	−0.016*	0.101***	0.093***
	(−8.28)	(7.01)	(−2.59)	(1.88)	(−1.89)	(47.89)	(23.65)
Log income	−0.087***	−0.019***	−0.018***	−0.000	0.006*	−0.001	−0.011***
	(−14.71)	(−4.05)	(−7.79)	(−0.08)	(1.91)	(−1.58)	(−7.91)
Log income*female	0.035***	0.017*	0.003	−0.003	−0.001	0.000	0.007***
	(3.81)	(1.68)	(0.65)	(−0.75)	(−0.19)	(0.27)	(3.08)
Tenure	0.013***	0.002*	0.001*				0.003***
	(18.23)	(1.81)	(1.95)				(14.62)
Tenure*female	0.002	0.000	0.002***				0.002***
	(1.43)	(0.20)	(4.90)				(6.82)
N	16,241	12,330	62,984	42,857	22,016	450,388	140,225

Note: t statistics in parentheses; decade dummies are included; (d) for discrete change of dummy variable from 0 to 1
*$p < 0.1$, **$p < 0.05$, ***$p < 0.01$

men—possibly suggesting that they are better off considering their engagement in building their wealth portfolio. Nevertheless, the positive sign of being a single woman does not offset the negative impact of being single, except in the UK where the two effects offset each other.

In a few northern and continental countries (Finland, Denmark, the Netherlands, Germany and France), income acts as a deterrent to homeownership for females. Thus, female renters do not seem to be more vulnerable despite the lack of housing assets. The effect of income for women is positive only in three countries (Belgium, Luxembourg and Canada).

The presence of children among single women reduces the likelihood of being homeowners only in Denmark, Canada and the US. In most other countries, being a single mother has no effect on owning your own home and is positive (Austria and Luxembourg). Most likely, this is due to favorable child custody laws and child allowances that are more generous toward women.

Worthy of note is the inclusion of the work tenure variable, in addition to income, in order to control for labor history and stability. Tenure, rather than income, seems to be more effective in shaping homeownership, and always impacts the ownership decision positively, albeit differentially for women. Tenure at work suggests stability, but it may also be that the causality runs in the other direction, as homeownership may induce people to stay in the same residence and thus at the same job. Conversely, income does differ in its impact across countries. Income has a positive effect in half of the cases, with the highest impact in absolute value is for Austria, where double income is associated with a decrease in probability of 9 ppt, while the highest positive value is for Denmark at 6 ppt.

3.8.2 Age Subgroups

Our unique data set allows us to observe whether the experiences of different cohorts have changed across the decades. It could very well be the case that the experiences of those born in the 1950s differ from those born in the 1970s. This can be observed to some extent in Fig. 3.3. In

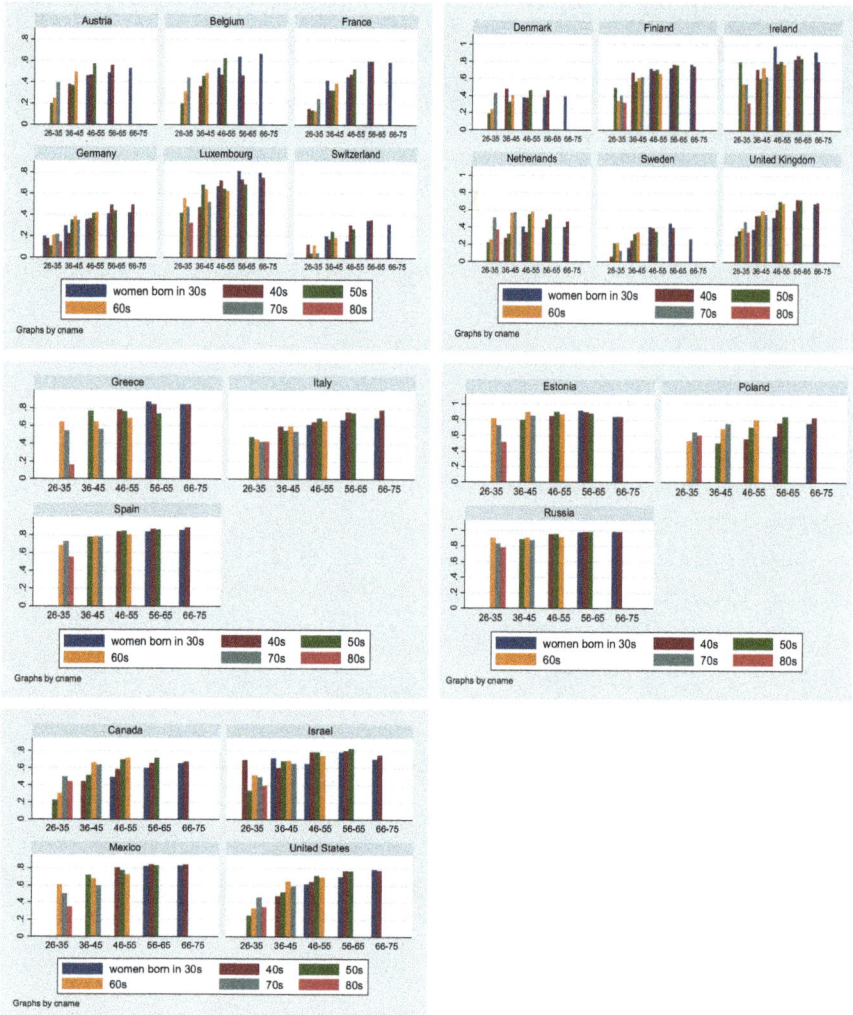

Fig. 3.3 Homeownership rates across different cohorts of female household heads. Source: LIS data; own calculations

many countries, women born in the 1970s seem to have very different homeownership experiences compared to women born earlier in the century—particularly among those in the youngest group (26–35 years old). In most countries, the younger cohort has a higher probability of owning their own home at this young age compared to the cohort born in the 1950s. This is the case in many Western European countries (except Switzerland), Canada and the US, but not so much in Southern European countries, Scandinavia and Ireland. Table 3.3 illustrates the results of the pooled regression for the younger cohort aged 25–45 for singles only. The results indicate that the negative effect for women remains in most countries even for the younger cohort. The negative effect for single mothers is present in almost all the countries and is statistically significant in 7 out of 14 countries.

The effect for women in the older cohort is more likely to be positive (Table 3.4) or insignificant. This is most likely due to the fact that women in this age group are more likely to be divorced or widowed, which would positively affect their probability of homeownership relatively to the never married category of single mothers.

3.8.3 Time Trend

Our results also control for a possible time trend effect, which may potentially vary in its impact on the gender dimension across countries. In the estimation, we include decade wave dummies and their interaction with the female (0/1) indicator to control for whether the decade effect had a differential impact on men and women. As indicated in Gabriel and Rosenthal (2013), in the 1990s the drivers of changes in homeownership rates principally included changes in socioeconomic and demographic attributes, while in the 2000–2010 period market conditions played a much larger role. To check the role of market conditions—whether, for example, the last recession had a more specific impact on the homeownership of women and men—we focus on decade dummies that are included in Table 3.3, our specification for the younger cohort. Our omitted category is the 1980s decade. The interaction between the yearly indicators and the female indicator shows that there were no significant changes over time in most countries. There are a few countries which are exceptions (Finland, Denmark and the UK). Looking at the older cohorts, those aged above 45, in Table 3.4, it is interesting to observe that looking at the time dummy after 2008, when

Table 3.3 Homeownership probit estimated for the pooled sample of waves for the cohort of 25–45 years old (marginal effects)

	Finland (1)	Denmark (2)	Netherlands (3)	UK (4)	Germany (5)	France (6)	Austria (7)
Female (d)	0.346***			−0.107	0.049	−0.029	−0.382***
	(3.38)			(−1.23)	(0.66)	(−0.38)	(−3.27)
Single + kids	0.092**	0.029	0.030	−0.079***	0.051*	0.058**	0.068
	(2.49)	(1.64)	(0.55)	(−3.40)	(1.80)	(2.23)	(1.24)
(Single + kids)*female	−0.124***	−0.082***	−0.123**	−0.091***	−0.020	−0.070***	−0.054
	(−3.08)	(−4.57)	(−2.34)	(−3.58)	(−0.77)	(−2.61)	(−0.99)
Age	0.085***	0.036***	0.089***	0.037***	0.054***	0.075***	0.039**
	(4.70)	(4.91)	(4.62)	(3.57)	(5.32)	(5.77)	(2.12)
Age2	−0.088***	−0.038***	−0.105***	−0.034**	−0.062***	−0.077***	−0.034
	(−3.56)	(−3.67)	(−3.90)	(−2.38)	(−4.44)	(−4.33)	(−1.33)
University degree	0.107***	0.043***	0.111***	0.165***	0.041***	0.081***	0.030
	(6.59)	(6.31)	(6.83)	(17.42)	(4.35)	(6.58)	(1.42)
Unemployed	−0.098**	0.140***	0.188***	−0.038	−0.026	−0.009	−0.157***
	(−2.47)	(6.25)	(2.75)	(−1.48)	(−0.95)	(−0.24)	(−2.92)
Unemployed*female	−0.016	−0.021	−0.025	0.088**	−0.068***	−0.015	0.118
	(−0.29)	(−0.77)	(−0.32)	(2.55)	(−2.64)	(−0.44)	(1.33)
Employed (d)	0.250***	0.269***	0.325***	0.375***	0.052***	0.111***	0.027
	(11.39)	(42.98)	(17.23)	(40.09)	(3.56)	(5.89)	(1.06)
Log income	0.043***	0.003	−0.014	−0.003	0.026***	0.014**	−0.059***
	(4.31)	(0.96)	(−0.94)	(−0.50)	(4.46)	(2.01)	(−5.48)
Log income*female	−0.040***	−0.033***	−0.013	0.003	−0.008	−0.000	0.045***
	(−3.05)	(−6.47)	(−0.64)	(0.40)	(−0.99)	(−0.02)	(3.29)
Tenure (work)	0.011***		0.013***	0.020***	0.005***		−0.001
	(3.00)		(3.11)	(14.36)	(5.21)		(−0.19)
Tenure*female	−0.007		0.001	0.002	−0.001		−0.006
	(−1.41)		(0.17)	(1.21)	(−0.79)		(−0.76)

(continued)

Table 3.3 (continued)

	Finland (1)	Denmark (2)	Netherlands (3)	UK (4)	Germany (5)	France (6)	Austria (7)
y1990 (d)	−0.058*		−0.184***	0.155***	−0.025	0.021	0.083***
	(−1.71)		(−5.55)	(3.48)	(−1.11)	(0.85)	(2.75)
y2000 (d)	−0.100***	0.003	−0.085***	0.114**	−0.041***	−0.019	−0.052
	(−2.76)	(0.20)	(−2.61)	(2.38)	(−2.97)	(−0.92)	(−1.30)
y2007 (d)	−0.071*		−0.053*	0.032	−0.012		
	(−1.82)		(−1.65)	(0.66)	(−0.65)		
y2010 (d)	−0.023	−0.109***		−0.031	−0.030*	−0.020	
	(−0.57)	(−6.88)		(−0.65)	(−1.71)	(−0.93)	
y1990*female (d)	−0.024	0.229***	0.024	0.081	−0.037	−0.025	−0.038
	(−0.52)	(4.01)	(0.15)	(1.36)	(−1.28)	(−0.83)	(−0.99)
y2000*female (d)	−0.092*	0.283***	0.077	0.117*	−0.014	0.004	0.030
	(−1.89)	(4.77)	(0.42)	(1.88)	(−0.73)	(0.14)	(0.55)
y2007*female (d)	−0.126**		0.044	0.140**	−0.036		
	(−2.46)		(0.24)	(2.23)	(−1.62)		
y2010*female (d)	−0.124**	0.248***	0.053	0.148**	−0.033	−0.010	
	(−2.34)	(4.17)	(0.29)	(2.36)	(−1.43)	(−0.34)	
N	5182	22,573	4115	17,301	8129	7120	4110

(continued)

Table 3.3 (continued)

	Luxembourg (8)	Belgium (9)	Italy (10)	Spain (11)	Greece (12)	US (13)	Canada (14)
Female (d)	0.112		−0.138		0.098	−0.106**	−0.236***
	(0.44)		(−0.62)		(0.41)	(−2.39)	(−3.13)
Single + kids	0.118	0.153*	0.065	0.024	−0.026	0.176***	0.123***
	(1.19)	(1.64)	(1.04)	(0.31)	(−0.21)	(20.27)	(7.23)
(Single + kids)*female	−0.111	−0.083	−0.091	−0.030	0.184	−0.141***	−0.085***
	(−1.13)	(−0.83)	(−1.43)	(−0.37)	(1.45)	(−14.44)	(−4.36)
Age	0.056*	0.021	0.014	0.138***	0.046	0.055***	0.044***
	(1.92)	(0.52)	(0.64)	(5.41)	(1.23)	(11.20)	(4.66)
Age2	−0.071*	0.000	−0.007	−0.166***	−0.045	−0.051***	−0.043***
	(−1.73)	(0.00)	(−0.21)	(−4.73)	(−0.84)	(−7.46)	(−3.27)
University degree	0.002	0.067*	0.193***	0.021	−0.016	0.098***	0.036***
	(0.07)	(1.93)	(8.37)	(0.98)	(−0.50)	(23.88)	(4.16)
Unemployed	−0.205**	0.107	−0.031	−0.093	−0.244**	0.066***	0.091***
	(−2.08)	(0.95)	(−0.40)	(−1.34)	(−2.52)	(4.09)	(3.72)
Unemployed*female	−0.029	−0.126	−0.212***	−0.025	0.161	−0.054***	−0.046
	(−0.22)	(−1.23)	(−3.35)	(−0.36)	(1.46)	(−3.06)	(−1.54)
Employed (d)	0.083	0.197***	−0.137***	0.014	−0.087	0.176***	0.186***
	(1.42)	(3.72)	(−3.54)	(0.35)	(−1.42)	(33.18)	(17.20)
Log income	−0.090***	−0.021	−0.028	0.005	−0.017	−0.005	−0.010
	(−3.90)	(−0.73)	(−1.37)	(0.30)	(−0.79)	(−1.57)	(−1.63)
Log income*female	−0.002	0.039	0.021	−0.017	−0.013	0.008**	0.014*
	(−0.06)	(1.08)	(0.80)	(−0.87)	(−0.43)	(2.02)	(1.70)
Tenure (work)	0.029***	0.011	0.009***				0.009***
	(7.72)	(1.57)	(4.20)				(6.59)
Tenure*female	−0.005	−0.000	−0.003				0.007***
	(−0.95)	(−0.05)	(−0.99)				(4.02)

(continued)

Table 3.3 (continued)

	Luxembourg (8)	Belgium (9)	Italy (10)	Spain (11)	Greece (12)	US (13)	Canada (14)
y1990 (d)			0.118***	−0.202***	0.099	0.018	−0.045*
			(2.65)	(−3.24)	(1.18)	(1.62)	(−1.79)
y2000 (d)	−0.110**	−0.025	0.037	−0.014	0.035	0.055***	0.010
	(−2.08)	(−0.32)	(0.73)	(−0.34)	(0.57)	(4.85)	(0.38)
y2007 (d)	−0.255***		0.025		0.006	0.050***	0.043
	(−4.94)		(0.44)		(0.10)	(3.80)	(1.44)
y2010 (d)	−0.125**		−0.012	0.026		0.032**	0.038
	(−2.07)		(−0.21)	(0.66)		(2.37)	(1.26)
y1990*female (d)	0.032	−0.341	−0.056	0.270***	−0.118	−0.017	0.019
	(0.39)	(−1.44)	(−0.98)	(2.75)	(−1.16)	(−1.21)	(0.55)
y2000*female (d)	0.037	−0.259	−0.021	0.120	−0.002	0.006	−0.020
	(0.57)	(−1.27)	(−0.32)	(0.78)	(−0.03)	(0.42)	(−0.57)
y2007*female (d)	0.003		−0.032	0.120	0.022	−0.026	−0.027
	(0.05)		(−0.45)	(0.77)	(0.26)	(−1.63)	(−0.70)
y2010*female (d)			−0.017	0.118		−0.019	−0.004
			(−0.24)	(0.74)		(−1.15)	(−0.11)
N	1995	1038	3323	2524	1195	62,580	17,301

Note: t statistics in parentheses; decade dummies are included; (d) for discrete change of dummy variable from 0 to 1
*$p < 0.1$, **$p < 0.05$, ***$p < 0.01$

Table 3.4 Homeownership probit estimates for the pooled sample of waves for the cohort of 45–65 years old (marginal effects)

	Finland (1)	Denmark (2)	Netherlands (3)	UK (4)	Germany (5)	France (6)	Austria (7)
Female (d)	0.154**	0.066*	−0.007	−0.012	0.083*	0.051	−0.259***
	(2.03)	(1.66)	(−0.08)	(−0.25)	(1.71)	(0.82)	(−3.53)
Single + kids	0.143***	0.060***	0.084***	0.003	0.191***	0.099***	0.118***
	(6.63)	(4.52)	(2.71)	(0.22)	(8.40)	(4.67)	(3.74)
Single + kids	−0.158***	−0.082***	−0.125***	−0.139***	−0.084***	−0.096***	−0.032
	(−5.64)	(−6.19)	(−3.91)	(−8.76)	(−4.44)	(−4.36)	(−0.94)
Age	0.033***	0.005***	0.019***	0.010***	0.021***	0.047***	0.035***
	(12.51)	(4.19)	(6.04)	(6.99)	(9.78)	(20.18)	(13.40)
Age2	−0.020***	0.005***	−0.010***	−0.001	−0.012***	−0.034***	−0.027***
	(−7.32)	(3.81)	(−3.31)	(−0.85)	(−5.43)	(−14.39)	(−10.82)
University degree	0.114***	0.077***	0.170***	0.128***	0.026***	0.127***	0.042**
	(11.36)	(16.06)	(15.73)	(21.72)	(3.53)	(11.91)	(2.40)
Unemployed	−0.145***	0.151***	−0.023	−0.080***	−0.115***	−0.126***	−0.183***
	(−5.97)	(9.51)	(−0.51)	(−4.53)	(−6.20)	(−5.28)	(−4.28)
Unemployed*female	0.033	−0.024	−0.013	0.055**	−0.026	0.006	0.071
	(1.03)	(−1.08)	(−0.22)	(2.26)	(−0.87)	(0.18)	(1.16)
Employed (d)	0.156***	0.303***	0.215***	0.319***	0.038***	0.037***	−0.011
	(11.91)	(60.79)	(15.03)	(46.82)	(3.63)	(3.06)	(−0.76)
Log income	0.029***	0.032***	−0.005	0.004	0.020***	0.029***	−0.079***
	(4.35)	(11.75)	(−0.56)	(1.14)	(4.40)	(4.82)	(−10.34)
Log income*female	−0.018**	−0.015***	−0.006	0.006	−0.014**	−0.012	0.029***
	(−2.10)	(−4.04)	(−0.56)	(1.18)	(−2.49)	(−1.60)	(3.21)
Tenure	0.004**		0.010***	0.008***	0.004***		0.004
	(2.53)		(3.93)	(13.10)	(6.01)		(0.89)
Tenure*female	−0.000		−0.002	0.003***	−0.002***		−0.007
	(−0.06)		(−0.74)	(3.77)	(−2.79)		(−1.19)

(continued)

Table 3.4 (continued)

	Finland (1)	Denmark (2)	Netherlands (3)	UK (4)	Germany (5)	France (6)	Austria (7)
y1990 (d)	−0.025 (−1.01)			0.232*** (9.64)	−0.028 (−1.18)	0.002 (0.10)	0.113*** (5.28)
y2000 (d)	−0.087*** (−3.50)	−0.044*** (−3.49)	0.131*** (5.05)	0.253*** (10.79)	0.012 (0.84)	−0.002 (−0.13)	−0.028 (−0.96)
y2007 (d)	−0.109*** (−4.06)		0.129*** (5.26)	0.213*** (8.75)	0.032* (1.81)		
y2010 (d)	−0.069** (−2.58)	−0.131*** (−10.34)	0.169*** (6.93)	0.213*** (8.75)	0.019 (1.16)	−0.060*** (−3.51)	
y1990*female (d)	0.002 (0.08)	−0.045*** (−2.65)	−0.027 (−0.90)	−0.011 (−0.36)	0.010 (0.34)	0.006 (0.23)	−0.015 (−0.60)
y2000*female (d)	−0.007 (−0.24)	0.019** (2.15)	−0.030 (−1.00)	0.009 (0.28)	0.006 (0.33)	0.029 (1.38)	−0.016 (−0.46)
y2007*female (d)	−0.012 (−0.36)			0.029 (0.91)	0.004 (0.18)		
y2010*female (d)	−0.054 (−1.56)		−0.016 (−0.56)	0.011 (0.34)	0.012 (0.56)	0.047** (2.12)	
N	13,594	55,833	10,279	43,665	22,037	18,023	12,613

(continued)

Table 3.4 (continued)

	Luxembourg (8)	Belgium (9)	Italy (10)	Spain (11)	Greece (12)	US (13)	Canada (14)
Female (d)	−0.213	−0.169	−0.041	0.060	0.080	0.019	−0.201***
	(−1.64)	(−1.13)	(−0.47)	(0.68)	(0.65)	(0.61)	(−4.06)
Single + kids	0.186***	0.136***	0.099***	0.054**	0.137***	0.200***	0.149***
	(4.35)	(2.80)	(4.39)	(2.25)	(3.53)	(31.01)	(12.63)
Single + kids	−0.177***	−0.142**	−0.054**	−0.036	−0.082	−0.161***	−0.077***
	(−3.50)	(−2.51)	(−2.06)	(−1.23)	(−1.53)	(−21.57)	(−5.45)
Age	−0.001	0.033***	0.028***	0.025***	0.023***	0.027***	0.016***
	(−0.20)	(5.82)	(9.33)	(8.86)	(5.69)	(32.87)	(9.99)
Age2	0.009*	−0.023***	−0.020***	−0.018***	−0.013***	−0.013***	−0.005***
	(1.85)	(−4.11)	(−7.10)	(−6.34)	(−3.34)	(−15.66)	(−3.15)
University degree	0.025	0.056**	0.172***	0.013	−0.001	0.120***	0.067***
	(1.36)	(2.48)	(12.44)	(1.17)	(−0.04)	(41.01)	(11.74)
Unemployed	−0.363***	−0.087	−0.098**	−0.099***	−0.101	0.018	−0.018
	(−5.92)	(−1.23)	(−2.10)	(−2.61)	(−1.56)	(1.58)	(−1.02)
Unemployed*female	0.074	−0.092	−0.072	−0.046	0.033	−0.059***	−0.004
	(0.82)	(−1.12)	(−1.21)	(−1.12)	(0.56)	(−4.04)	(−0.15)
Employed (d)	−0.038	0.087***	−0.076***	0.001	−0.050**	0.141***	0.133***
	(−1.35)	(2.83)	(−4.49)	(0.08)	(−2.30)	(38.20)	(17.74)
Log income	−0.099***	−0.034**	−0.025***	−0.001	−0.002	−0.001	−0.012***
	(−6.64)	(−2.02)	(−2.84)	(−0.09)	(−0.13)	(−0.32)	(−2.81)
Log income*female	0.052***	0.033	0.001	−0.004	−0.003	0.001	0.012**
	(2.85)	(1.58)	(0.08)	(−0.41)	(−0.23)	(0.45)	(2.22)
Tenure	0.013***	0.008**	0.003***				0.005***
	(7.96)	(2.24)	(2.99)				(7.24)
Tenure*female	−0.001	−0.002	0.000				0.003***
	(−0.29)	(−0.53)	(0.25)				(4.10)

(continued)

Table 3.4 (continued)

	Luxembourg (8)	Belgium (9)	Italy (10)	Spain (11)	Greece (12)	US (13)	Canada (14)
y1990 (d)		-0.053	0.018	-0.062*	0.093**	0.018**	-0.046**
		(-1.16)	(0.63)	(-1.91)	(2.51)	(2.07)	(-2.45)
y2000 (d)	-0.039		0.040	-0.007	0.050	0.040***	-0.008
	(-0.96)		(1.33)	(-0.34)	(1.57)	(4.59)	(-0.41)
y2007 (d)	-0.186***		0.062*		-0.036	0.031***	-0.002
	(-4.17)		(1.90)		(-1.08)	(3.29)	(-0.12)
y2010 (d)	-0.044		0.026	0.012		0.014	-0.012
	(-1.00)		(0.78)	(0.59)		(1.44)	(-0.59)
y1990*female (d)	-0.031		-0.018	0.040	-0.100*	-0.009	0.025
	(-0.54)		(-0.53)	(1.23)	(-1.72)	(-0.89)	(1.06)
y2000*female (d)	-0.018	-0.047	0.025	-0.000	-0.041	0.001	0.005
	(-0.41)	(-0.84)	(0.69)	(-0.02)	(-0.99)	(0.09)	(0.21)
y2007*female (d)			0.010	0.002	0.016	-0.024**	0.006
			(0.25)	(0.06)	(0.41)	(-2.05)	(0.22)
y2010*female (d)	-0.059		0.041			-0.022*	0.025
	(-1.29)		(1.03)			(-1.83)	(0.95)
N	4501	2961	13,404	8803	4445	137,851	38,933

Note: t statistics in parentheses; decade dummies are included; (d) for discrete change of dummy variable from 0 to 1
*$p < 0.1$, **$p < 0.05$, ***$p < 0.01$

the crisis hit, we do not find any difference in the sign of that decade compared to the previous ones. The crisis did not change the general long-running trend. The only exception is in the US where the positive trend stopped and in France, which has a negative association after 2008. The interaction with the female indicator variable is almost always not significant with the exception of France after the crisis: the positive sign of the interaction suggests that the crisis mostly affected men as the negative effect is almost offset for women. Conversely, in the US the gap between women and men has increased over the last decade, as the crisis did not reverse the trend. Looking now at the new demographic inflows, we notice more dynamics going on in the gender gap. In Finland, women have substantially lowered their probability of becoming homeowners over time, whereas in the UK, women are those driving the increasing trend in homeownership over time. The crisis seems to have shaped differently the ongoing time trend and the gender gap in only a few countries.

3.9   Discussion

The benefits linked to homeownership are certainly high from a welfare point of view and in order to dilute risk. For a certain population of owners, particularly those in old age, homeownership is a tool against the risk of poverty. Housing equity is part of total wealth and thus guarantees that people can rely upon some wealth in case of surprises and have access to borrowing by putting their housing up as collateral.

Looking at housing as a saving mechanism, subscribing to a mortgage (endowment mortgage) constitutes an "easy" way to accumulate wealth since everybody needs a place to live, and by satisfying this necessity, households can accumulate wealth, as we will elaborate in more detail in Chap. 4. This is a quite unique feature of housing unlike other essential goods such as health-related expenditures, and it is also a chance for investment and savings. Homeowners are essentially saving by paying off their mortgages and consequently increasing their home equity. By having a strong commitment to mortgage, households are effectively forced to save *more* than they would otherwise. In this way, their accumulated housing wealth can also play an additional role and be used as collateral when it comes to borrowing, and in the face of borrowing constraints. From an intertemporal perspective, household future well-being (e.g. measured by consumption) is determined not only by wealth and investment opportunities, but also by future net income if a household is borrowing constrained.

3.10 Concluding Remarks

The status of homeowner belongs to a vast majority of the population, with the exception of Germany and Austria, where the median household does not have the status of homeowner. Apart from ex-communist countries where the homeownership rate has been inflated by converting previously rented flats to owned flats, the percentage of homeowners rarely exceeds 80%, thus suggesting that a 20% floor of non-owners might be the physiological rate of renting. This could be due to poverty and also due to natural demographic factors. For example, at a young age, renting can be optimal to allow for mobility and search opportunities for better jobs, which might necessitate moving. At retirement, liquidating assets is also part of the optimality patters.

With respect to the family and gender dimensions, we can see that family type rather than gender determines the decision of homeownership. In particular, single households are less likely to be homeowners, thus exposing them to the risk of having zero housing equity and not having equity to rely upon in case of need. The risk is, however, reduced for single women, who are more inclined to own their home compared to single men.

From a policy standpoint, the incentive of homeownership seems particularly important for these household types.

Appendix

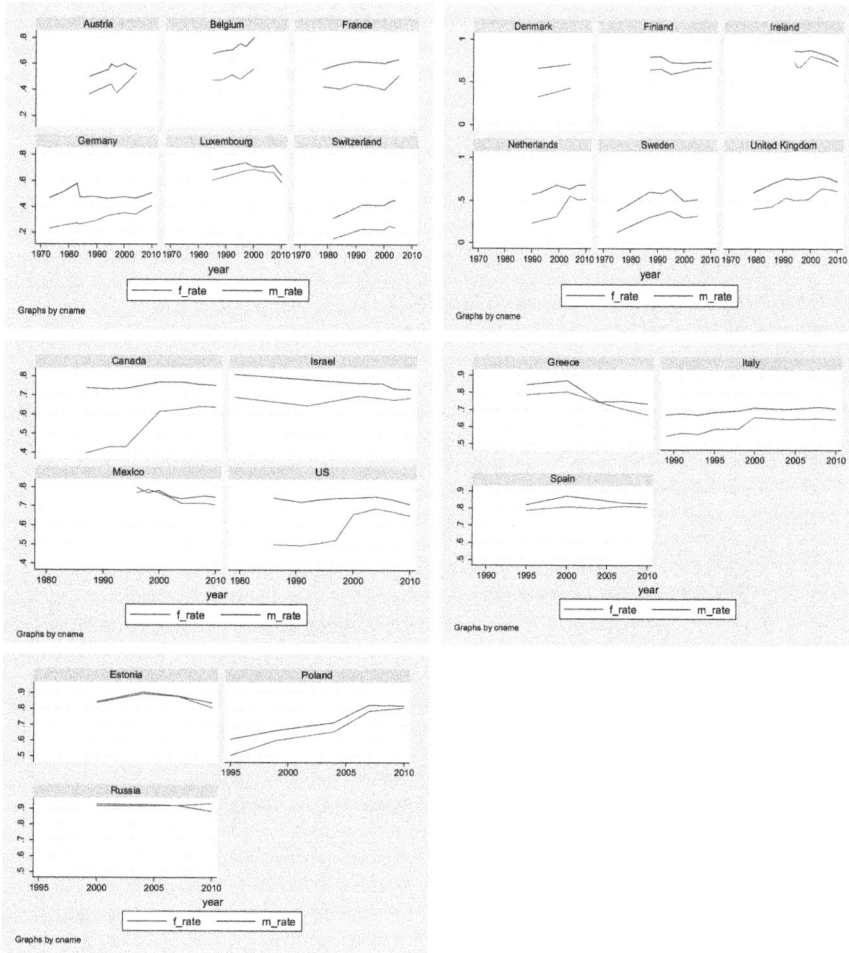

Fig. 3.4 Homeownership by gender of the household head. Source: LIS data; own calculations

Families and Housing Decisions: A Look Across OECD Countries

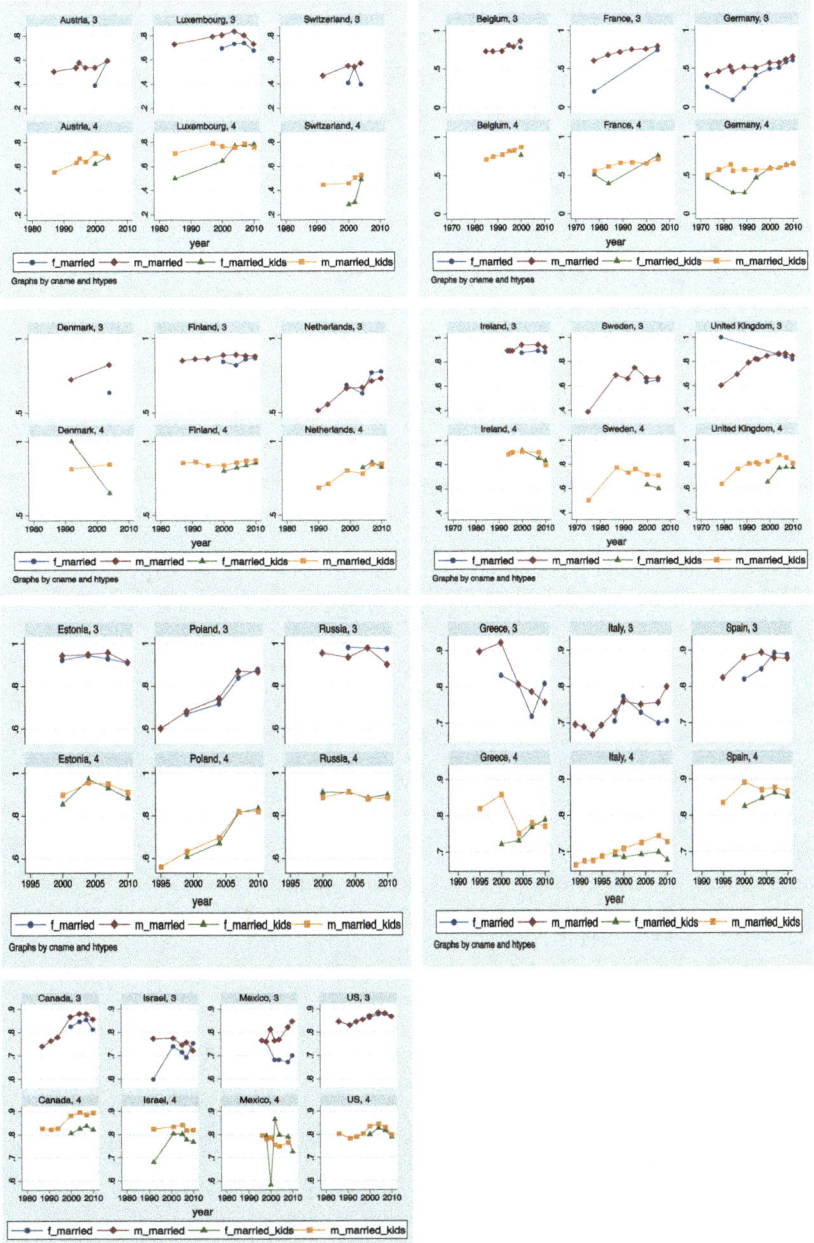

Fig. 3.5 Homeownership rates by family type over the decades (for married and married with kids). Source: LIS data; own elaboration

Table 3.5 Data availability in our selected countries in the LIS database

Waves	0	1	2	3	4	5	6	7	8
Austria			87		94/95/97	00	04		
Belgium			85	88/92	95/97	00			
Canada	71	75/81	87	91	94/97	98/00	04	07	10
Switzerland		81		92		00	02/04		
Germany	73	78/81	83/84	89	94	00	04	07	10
Denmark				92	95	00	04		
Estonia						00	04	07	10
Spain		80	85	90	95	00	04	07	10
Finland			87	91	95	00	04	07	10
France		78	84	89	94	00	05		10
Greece					95	00	04	07	10
Ireland			87		94/95/96	00		07	10
Israel		79		92	97	00	05	07	10
Italy			86/87	89/91	93/95	98/00	04	08	10
Luxembourg			85		97	00	04	07	10
Mexico			84	89/92	94/96	98/00	02/04	08	10
Netherlands			83/87	90	93	99	04	07	10
Poland			86	92	95	99	04	07	10
Russia						00	04	07	10
Sweden		75/81	87	92	95	00	05		
UK	69/73	79	86	91	94/95	99	04	07	10
US	74	79	86	91	94/97	00	04	07	10

Source: LIS Datacenter website

Table 3.6 Variables used in the estimation

Variable names	Definitions
Female (d)	0/1 indicator: 0 = male; 1 = female
Single (d)	0/1 indicator: 1 = 1-person household; 0 = otherwise
Single + kids	0/1 indicator: 1 = 1-person household with children under 18; 0 = otherwise
Married (d)	0/1 indicator: 1 = 2-person household married; 0 = otherwise
Married + kids	0/1 indicator: 1 = 2-person household married with children under 18; 0 = otherwise
Cohabiting	0/1 indicator: 1 = 2-person household not married; 0 = otherwise
Cohabiting + kids	0/1 indicator: 1 = 2-person household not married with children under 18; 0 = otherwise
Age	Age of respondent
University degree	0/1 indicator: respondent obtained university degree
Unemployed	0/1 indicator: respondent in unemployed
Employed (d)	0/1 indicator: respondent in employed
Log income	Log of household disposable income
Tenure	Years worked at current job

Source: LIS data; own elaboration

Table 3.7 LIS datacenter source surveys

Country	Years	Survey (English)
Austria	87/95	Microcensus
	94/97/00	European Community Household Panel (ECHP)
	04	Survey on Income and Living Conditions (SILC)
Belgium	85/88/92/97	Socio-Economic Panel (SEP)
	95/00	Panel Study on Belgian Households (PSBH)/ECHP
Canada	87/91/94	Survey of Consumer Finances (SCF)
	00/04/07/10	Survey of Labour and Income Dynamics (SLID)
Denmark	92/04	Law Model
Finland	87/91/95/00	Income Distribution Survey (IDS)
	04/07/10	IDS/SILC
France	78/84/89/94/00/05/10	Household Budget Survey (BdF)
Germany	73/78/83	Income and Consumer Survey (EVS)
	84/89/94/00/04/07/10	German Socio-Economic Panel (GSOEP)
Luxembourg	85	Socio-Economic Panel "Living in Luxembourg" (PSELL I)
	97/00	PSELL II/ECHP
	04/07/10	PSELL III/SILC
Switzerland	82	Swiss Income and Wealth Survey
	92	National Poverty Study
	00/02/04	Income and Expenditure Survey (ERC/EVE)
US	74/86/91/94/97/00	Current Population Survey (CPS)—March Supplement
	04/07/10	CPS—Annual Social and Economic Supplement (ASEC)
Greece	95/00	ECHP
	04/07/10	SILC
Ireland	94/95/96/00	Living in Ireland Survey/ECHP
	07/10	SILC
Israel	79/92/01/05/07/10	Household Expenditure Survey
Italy	89/91/93/95/98/00/04/08/10	Survey of Household Income and Wealth (SHIW)
Mexico	96/98/00/02/04/08/10	Household Income and Expenditure Survey (ENIGH)
Netherlands	90	Amenities and Services Utilization Survey (AVO)
	93/99	Socio-Economic Panel Survey (SEP)

(continued)

Table 3.7 (continued)

Country	Years	Survey (English)
	04/07/10	SILC
Spain	95/00	ECHP
	04/07/10	SILC
Sweden	75/87/92/95/00/05	Income Distribution Survey (HINK)
UK	79/86/91/95	Family Expenditure Survey (FES)
	94/99/04/07/10	Family Resources Survey (FRS)
Estonia	00	Household Budget Survey
	04/07/10	Estonian Social Survey (ESS)/SILC
Poland	95/99/04/07/10	Household Budget Survey
Russia	00/04/07/10	Russia Longitudinal Monitoring Survey (RLMS)

Table 3.8 Household structure across countries by waves

	Years	Single (%)	Single parents (%)	Couples (%)	Couples with kids (%)	%
Austria						
Wave 1	1987	24	8	27	42	100
Wave 2	1994–1995–1997	19	7	24	50	100
Wave 3	2000–2004	19	7	25	49	100
Belgium						
Wave 1	1985	8	3	29	59	100
Wave 2	1988–1992–1995–1997	12	4	30	54	100
Wave 3	2000	17	5	30	48	100
Canada						
Wave 1	1987	10	8	25	57	100
Wave 2	1991–1994	14	6	29	52	100
Wave 3	2000–2004	18	6	29	46	100
Wave 4	2007	21	7	30	42	100
Wave 5	2010	20	8	30	43	100
Denmark						
Wave 2	1992	25	4	31	40	100
Wave 3	2004	25	4	35	36	100
Finland						
Wave 1	1987	15	3	29	53	100
Wave 2	1991–1995	16	3	33	49	100
Wave 3	2000–2004	16	3	39	42	100
Wave 4	2007	16	2	42	40	100
Wave 5	2010	18	2	42	38	100
France						
Wave 1	1978–1984	14	3	29	54	100

(continued)

Table 3.8 (continued)

	Years	Single (%)	Single parents (%)	Couples (%)	Couples with kids (%)	%
Wave 2	1989–1994	16	4	31	50	100
Wave 3	2000–2005	18	4	34	44	100
Germany						
Wave 1	1973–1978–1983–1984	9	2	34	55	100
Wave 2	1989–1994	10	3	33	54	100
Wave 3	2000–2004	11	2	40	47	100
Wave 4	2007	14	2	41	43	100
Wave 5	2010	16	2	42	40	100
Luxembourg						
Wave 1	1985	15	6	28	51	100
Wave 2	1997	20	7	23	50	100
Wave 3	2000–2004	21	6	26	47	100
Wave 4	2007	23	5	23	49	100
Wave 5	2010	21	5	24	50	100
Switzerland						
Wave 1	1982					
Wave 2	1992	7	1	33	58	100
Wave 3	2000–2002–2004	14	2	37	47	100
US						
Wave 1	1974–1986	15	7	31	47	100
Wave 2	1991–1994–1997	18	7	31	44	100
Wave 3	2000–2004	20	7	32	41	100
Wave 4	2007	21	7	33	39	100
Wave 5	2010	22	7	33	37	100
Greece						
Wave 2	1995	18	5	26	51	100
Wave 3	2000–2004	15	7	25	53	100
Wave 4	2007	13	8	21	59	100
Wave 5	2010	11	7	21	60	100
Ireland						
Wave 2	1994–1995–1996	19	5	17	59	100
Wave 3	2000	18	9	17	56	100
Wave 4	2007	20	13	22	45	100
Wave 5	2010	20	9	25	45	100
Israel						
Wave 1	1979					
Wave 2	1992	14	7	17	62	100
Wave 3	2001–2005	11	7	16	66	100
Wave 4	2007	11	8	16	65	100
Wave 5	2010	11	8	16	65	100
Italy						
Wave 2	1989–1991–1993–1995	11	6	20	63	100

(continued)

Table 3.8 (continued)

	Years	Single (%)	Single parents (%)	Couples (%)	Couples with kids (%)	%
Wave 3	1998–2000–2004	15	6	23	56	100
Wave 4	2008	19	6	25	50	100
Wave 5	2010	17	6	26	50	100
Mexico						
Wave 2	1996	7	11	7	75	100
Wave 3	1998–2000–2002–2004	8	12	9	70	100
Wave 4	2008	10	13	11	66	100
Wave 5	2010	12	14	13	61	100
Netherlands						
Wave 2	1990–1993	14	3	28	56	100
Wave 3	1999–2004	17	2	31	50	100
Wave 4	2007	17	3	31	49	100
Wave 5	2010	19	3	33	45	100
Spain						
Wave 2	1995	12	8	20	60	100
Wave 3	2000–2004	14	8	22	56	100
Wave 4	2007	15	7	21	57	100
Wave 5	2010	17	8	22	53	100
Sweden						
Wave 1	1975–1987	10	1	43	46	100
Wave 2	1992–1995	16	2	44	38	100
Wave 3	2000–2005	10	3	42	45	100
UK						
Wave 1	1979–1986	16	5	30	49	100
Wave 2	1991–1994–1995	21	6	32	41	100
Wave 3	1999–2004	24	7	33	36	100
Wave 4	2007	26	8	32	34	100
Wave 5	2010	26	8	32	34	100
Estonia						
Wave 3	2000–2004	22	11	26	41	100
Wave 4	2007	26	10	27	37	100
Wave 5	2010	25	9	28	38	100
Poland						
Wave 2	1995	16	4	24	56	100
Wave 3	2000–2004	16	6	24	55	100
Wave 4	2007	19	6	22	53	100
Wave 5	2010	20	4	23	52	100
Russia						
Wave 3	2000–2004	26	12	22	40	100
Wave 4	2007	30	15	21	34	100
Wave 5	2010	29	15	21	35	100

Notes

1. One of the explanations for differentiated homeownership rates could be institutional regimes. For a discussion of these consult Wind et al. (2016).
2. The issue of changing preferences and asset ownership is addressed to some extent in Rossi and Sierminska (2015). A discussion on the distribution of assets in a household is discussed in Grabka et al. (2015).

References

Belsky, E. (2009). Demographics, markets, and future of housing demand. *Journal of Housing Research, 18*(2), 99–119.

Chambers, M. S., Schlangenhauf, D. E., & Young, E. R. (2003). *Are husbands really that cheap? Exploring life insurance holdings.* Manuscript, Florida State University.

Dillingh, R., Prast, H., Rossi, M., & Brancati, C. U. (2017). Who wants to have their home and eat it too? Interest in reverse mortgages in the Netherlands. *Journal of Housing Economics, 38*, 25–37.

Gabriel, S. A., & Rosenthal, S. S. (2013). Urbanization, agglomeration economies, and access to mortgage credit. *Regional Science and Urban Economics, 43*, 42–50.

Grabka, M., Marcus, J., & Sierminska, E. (2015). Wealth distribution within couples. *Review of Economics of the Household, 13*(3), 459–486. https://doi.org/10.1007/s11150-013-9229-2.

Haurin, D. R., Parcel, T. L., & Haurin, R. J. (2002). Does homeownership affect child outcomes? *Real Estate Economics, 30*(4), 635–666.

Luxembourg Income Study (LIS) Database. (2016). http://www.lisdatacenter.org (multiple countries; 1971–2010). Luxembourg: LIS.

McGinn, D. (2013). How single women—And what they want—Are shaping the new housing market. *The Globe and Mail.*

Oswald, A. J. (1996). *A conjecture on the explanation for high unemployment in the industrialized nations: Part I.* Warwick Economics Research Paper Series (TWERPS), 475.

Rossi, M., & Sierminska, E. (2015). *Single again? Saving patterns when widowhood occurs.* Netspar Discussion Paper No. 02/2015-004. https://doi.org/10.2139/ssrn.2569127.

Wind, B., Lersch, P. M., & Dewilde, C. (2016). The distribution of housing wealth in 16 European countries: Accounting for institutional differences. *Journal of Housing and the Built Environment,* Published Online.

4

Homeownership and Wealth Accumulation

Abstract This chapter elaborates on the relationship between homeownership and wealth, particularly investigating whether homeowners have additional wealth, which seems to be the case. We run the empirical analysis using the Household Finance and Consumption Survey (HFCS) data for two waves and point to differences that exist among women and men. The chapter also questions the risks that an excessively illiquid portfolio might generate.

Keywords Homeownership and wealth • Housing • Life cycle

4.1 Introduction

The importance of housing wealth at the household level, as well as in the economy as a whole, is indisputable. Housing wealth represents a major component of wealth in several countries and housing expenditures have accounted for more than one-fifth of the US GDP over the past 50 years.

We are thankful to Mario Cannella for invaluable research assistance using the HFCS data and to an anonymous referee for useful and thoughtful suggestions on this chapter.

© The Author(s) 2018
M. Rossi, E. M. Sierminska, *Wealth and Homeownership*,
https://doi.org/10.1007/978-3-319-92558-5_4

Since fewer people are having children in the EU and the US of late, this could suggest a decreasing need of owning an accommodation for prudential reasons, but homeownership keeps rising. As highlighted in Chap. 3, at the moment, about two-thirds of European households are owners of the household they live in (Elsinga et al. 2012).

Housing wealth also acts as a key player in influencing economic choices. The literature on consumption and saving patterns has shown that consumption choices are affected by investment in housing wealth. More importantly, and somehow surprisingly given the illiquid form of housing wealth, consumption reacts more to housing wealth than to financial wealth capital gains (Belsky and Prakken 2004; Takhtamanova and Sierminska 2012; Calcagno et al. 2009). Perhaps this is due to the fact that housing wealth is less volatile than stock wealth, as its decline or increase cannot change rapidly. It thus adds stability to the stock of wealth owned by households by representing an anchor for household wealth.

Housing and the labor market are also intertwined. The literature is not unanimous regarding the effect of housing tenure on labor market outcomes, particularly in relation to unemployment duration. Oswald's (1996) conjecture is that a high level of homeownership might be responsible for the high unemployment rate by limiting the search initiative of employees to the boundaries of their area of residence.[1]

Most households have the majority of their investments embedded in a house and for some of them housing equity is the only available capital (Horsewood and Neuteboom 2006). Remarkably, very little is known in the economic literature about the optimal amount and timing of house purchases.

Housing wealth is, however, very difficult to investigate, particularly when focusing on optimality. What is the optimal amount of housing wealth? Do households have too much of it, leading to overaccumulation? Housing investments are complicated, as homeowners cannot easily be disentangled from housing services. Overall, housing is a unique form of wealth.

In this chapter, we intend to focus on the question of whether housing acts as a driver of total wealth accumulation. Moreover, we want to focus on whether women show a higher or lower level of wealth controlling for homeownership, along with other explanatory variables such as education and family types. Descriptive evidence shows that homeowners exhibit a higher level of wealth. Using econometric analysis, we examine whether this channel is at work, once other variables of control are considered.

To develop this idea, we draw on data from the Household Finance and Consumption Survey. This is a new and comprehensive data source that has substantial value in cross-country comparative wealth research. Our results corroborate the descriptive evidence and show a positive and significant correlation between wealth and homeownership. Moreover, women seem to be, in several countries, more propense to wealth accumulation, a result which is consolidating the evidence provided by Rossi and Sierminska (2015) for US widows.

One point to stress when evaluating housing equity and its importance is that survey values of housing equity are self-declared, meaning that, on average, the value is above the actual price a household would be able to fetch for its dwelling. Put differently, housing value is likely to be overstated by owners, and the housing value recorded with an upward bias. Indeed, all the differences in housing wealth, which basically drives differences in wealth across EU countries, can be more realistically reduced, if housing were evaluated at the price at which each owned house could be reasonably sold within the interview year. The upward bias in housing equity could be responsible for a higher return rate of housing than the actual one, leading, in turn, to an overinvestment in housing equity by households. An overinvestment driven by the myth of housing wealth being a "superior" investment (Romiti and Rossi 2014). As the Nobel Prize winner Shiller highlights, investing in housing is believed to be a strong investment by Americans, but this belief is not based on facts. Looking at the history of the housing market, it hasn't been a good provider of capital gains. Housing, Shiller explains, is a good provider of housing services, but not a good provider of capital gains, despite American households believing the opposite (Shiller 2007; USA Today 2014). Nevertheless, the discussion continues as returns vary depending on such factors as purchase timing, holding period and location (Goodman and Mayer 2018).

The US evidence also indicates that homeowners amass greater wealth than renters (Belsky and Prakken 2004). A typical homeowner has wealth of $167,000 (USD) versus $42,000 for the typical renter over the of 1984–1999 time range. Marital status and age are only partially responsible for that gap. The longer the housing tenure, the higher the wealth gap, as highlighted by Li and Yang (2010), and Liu; this evidence shows a strongly positive correlation between housing tenure and accumulated wealth. The higher level of accumulation could be due to the endogeneity of homeowners, homeowners having a greater propensity to accumulate wealth than tenants in the first place. Putting it differently, the relationship between homeownership and higher wealth cannot be claimed to be causal. Being a homeowner is, in fact, a decision in itself, which is, in turn, driven by a higher propensity for accumulation. Finding a positive association between homeownership and wealth could just be capturing the propensity for accumulation of the household, making the causality claim difficult to prove.[2]

The main mechanism through which housing is an easier asset to accumulate compared to others is via mortgage (capital) repayments, which force households to adhere to a payment scheme as a sort of mandatory saving scheme. This channel effectively forces households to save more than they would without the mortgage scheme. If this channel of savings is indeed at work, further research is needed to investigate the long-term consequences of overinvestment in housing. Using a behavioral economics perspective, we can consider that wealth tied into housing equity (which is paid off using a mortgage loan) is a commitment device that cannot be consumed, precisely because of its illiquid nature (Laibson 1997). Recently, after the financial crisis, the usefulness and dangers of mortgages have been looked at more carefully. Mortgage and housing decisions are likely to be affected by the lack of self-control and myopia among households (Schlafmann 2016). Households showing a higher rate of self-control will either own smaller houses or less likely be homeowners. For people with a lack of self-control, regulation of mortgages could be useful and welfare enhancing. This could be done by reducing the availability of subprime mortgages that require a low down payment, for example. In the absence of self-control problems, a mortgage could serve as a commitment for saving, although it will be uninfluential in some sense, as rational individuals will save their optimal amount anyway.

4.2 Wealth and Housing: A Life Cycle Perspective

In Chap. 1, we have illustrated the basic economic conceptual framework provided by the life cycle permanent income (LCPI) model (Modigliani and Brumberg 1954; Friedman 1957; Deaton 1992), which provides the background in understanding how decisions on how much to consume and how much to devote to savings (postponed consumption) are made.

Net asset[3] value evolves according to the following well-known identity:

$$A_t = (1+r_t) A_{t-1} + y_t - c_t. \tag{4.1}$$

In more analytical terms, households are supposed to maximize their utility function as follows:

$$\max U(c_1, c_2, \ldots, c_T),$$

where c_t is the consumption in year t; T indicates the working lifetime span ending (with certainty) in year T. The household maximizes its (intertemporal) utility, which is based on consumption only. Consumption is a composite good and comprises food expenditure and services, including housing services. The household is subject to a budget constraint, as shown in Eq. (4.1). The terminal value of wealth at death (the year T) is zero, as there is no utility associated with wealth after death and Ponzi games (dying in debt) are not allowed.

The logic provided in the LCPI hypothesis, described in detail in Chap. 1, is very clear: as there is no value in assets after death, households should consume all their resources and exhibit no extra assets at death. According to the LCPI model, after retirement, when assets peaks, households should optimally decumulate resources.

Since households are supposed to maximize a utility function based on consumption, as the neoclassical economic theory postulates, convex preferences generate a profile of consumption smoothing over time. According to Modigliani's life cycle hypothesis (LCH), individuals smooth their lifetime consumption by borrowing when "young," saving when "middle aged" and dissaving when "old." Different stages in life are therefore characterized by different saving/dissaving patterns according to whether the current income is higher/lower than the permanent income.

Studying how total net wealth evolves is not a simple task. In fact, it involves considering each component's trajectory, of which the determinants of ownership vary widely. For example, climbing on to the property ladder is driven by different factors from those regarding holding stocks, which are in turn different from the determinants of owning bonds. Keeping this in mind, let us now examine the two main components of current net wealth that are responsible for accumulation over time.

Where is housing wealth in the accumulation process?

Housing is considered a non-financial (illiquid) asset. How assets are decomposed into financial and non-financial assets can be considered a portfolio decision, so can the decision to allocate financial wealth to risky and riskless assets. While considerable research has focused on how to allocate a portfolio optimally, little is known about the optimal amount of housing (Calcagno et al. 2009).

The question of whether housing equity could have reached a level that is too high is not new to the empirical literature. Although being a homeowner neutralizes the risk of being exposed to rental price variability on the one hand, it also imposes illiquidity costs and generates more costs for mobility on the other hand (e.g. see Romiti and Rossi 2014; Sinai and Souleles 2005).

As anticipated in Chap. 3, the role of mortgages in building up housing assets cannot be neglected. Mortgages have witnessed a rapid and constant increase over time (Bokhari et al. 2013). Between 1985 and 2007, the share of household mortgage debt as a proportion of the total housing value increased substantially from 30% to 50% in the US. Contemporaneously, housing prices increased, which implies that the amount borrowed also increased. Bokhari et al.'s (2013) results show that greater house prices lead borrowers not only to borrow more but also to buy more expensive houses. Although this kept leverage virtually unchanged, the consequence was a rise in households' risk exposure. This is because, controlling for income, a high loan amount implies a higher loan-to-income ratio. This amounts to a greater debt service and exposure to greater risk of illiquidity in the future. We also find that, in markets with greater house price volatility, both borrowers and lenders contracted at lower LTV ratios, which is consistent with the theory.

4.3 Financial Knowledge and Education. Do They Matter for Homeownership?

Financial knowledge could represent one important factor in shaping portfolio and wealth accumulation. Indeed, the financial knowledge of a household is likely to support all financial decisions with consciousness and sound knowledge.

As highlighted by Borella and Rossi (2014), financial knowledge has been advocated as one of the most relevant factors affecting saving patterns as well as balanced portfolio decisions (Van Rooij et al. 2012). Financial literacy is also responsible for fostering homeownership (as shown in several papers by Mitchell et al. 1999), as better-educated people are more likely to climb the homeownership ladder. In addition, financially literate individuals might be more efficient in their portfolio choices, generating higher returns from their savings and being able to accumulate more wealth. As a consequence, financial literacy is associated with better planning for retirement and with higher levels of wealth at the time of retirement.

While much has been written on accumulation and financial literacy, little has been found on the later stages of the life cycle: the decumulation phase. One exception is represented by Romiti and Rossi (2014), who point out that more effective use of personal wealth determines a higher welfare level of the elderly. Financial literacy should be responsible for a better decumulation pattern, as well as having been found to be responsible for a higher accumulation pace. Financial literacy enables households to gain deeper knowledge and understanding of complex financial products, such as reverse mortgages, which enable households to draw on the wealth accumulated in housing and end their life with the desired level of wealth (which could be zero or positive with the exact amount of bequests). In this way, they are more aware of the available options to make better use of their assets and the value of bequest would be the wanted one, rather than unintended bequest (Warshawsky 2018).

The "art of decumulation" should also depend on financial awareness, the life cycle predicting that financial knowledge should foster wealth decumulation after retirement (Van der Schors et al. 2007; Chiuri and Jappelli 2010).

4.4 The Household Finance and Consumption Survey Data Set

The Eurosystem Household Finance and Consumption Survey (HFCS), run by the European Central Bank, was first published in 2013. The data set, currently consisting of two waves, contains cross-sectional household-level data from 15 Euro area countries, collecting about 62,000 households interviewed for the first time in 2009/2010.

The HFCS provides ex ante comparable data for the Euro area countries. It includes information regarding sociodemographic variables, assets, liabilities, income and consumption for a sample of households that is representative both at the national and at the Euro area level. A set of population weights is provided to ensure the representativeness of the sample.

Another important feature of the HFCS is that missing observations for all the variables that are necessary to construct wealth and income aggregates (i.e. questions that were not answered by the respondent households) are imputed five times—an issue that we will take into account when assessing the statistical significance of our estimates. The HFCS data refer to 2008 in Spain, 2009 in Finland, Greece and the Netherlands and 2010 in all the remaining countries.

Table 4.1 illustrates the homeownership rates across EU countries for both available waves and for different family types: female and male *singles* with or without children and *couples* with or without children. The evidence emerging clearly shows that there is virtually no difference, at the aggregate level, for couples with or without children in housing tenure, while single people with or without children show larger differences: women, in particular, are those with lower incidence of housing tenure.

Table 4.1 Family types, homeownership and net wealth

	Whole sample		
	Net wealth	Net wealth-homeowners	Homeownership
Single-parents*female	74,340	183,071	36%
Single-parents*male	271,425	426,149	60%
Single no kids female	129,588	221,821	51%
Single no kids*male	139,576	261,826	44%
Couples with kids	242,145	313,393	72%
Couples no kids	263,139	337,848	73%

Source: Elaboration on HFCS data

Cross-tabulating the homeownership dimension with the average value of wealth, a clear pattern emerges across different types of families: homeowners are richer than renters across all types of families, as illustrated in Table 4.1. The descriptive evidence for the EU, as well as the US, shows that homeowners are on average richer than renters.

What could be the reason? Homeowners could be more oriented toward asset accumulation and hence will exhibit greater wealth overall in the long run. However, the endogeneity of homeownership could also be leading this effect. Homeowners are naturally more inclined to save; hence, they exhibit a higher level of accumulation. In the absence of arbitrage, the two choices should be equivalent. For example, a renter could invest the same amount of money that a homeowner repays in the mortgage capital repayment scheme and as a result accumulate the same amount of capital.

As shown in Fig. 4.1 and confirmed in the following panel regression analysis, age unsurprisingly plays a big role for all types of families. Aging is indeed associated with the accumulation peak. Older households have a higher rate of homeownership. The only exception is single women without children, probably reflecting a cohort effect. Single aged women do not have the same features as single young women, who seem to be more successful than single young men without children. Aged single individuals with children show a higher incidence of homeownership after 75; this fact probably absorbs the widowhood effect. A more detailed discussion can be found in Chap. 3.

In a recent paper, Kaas et al. (2016) show that households that are homeowners are richer than renters in Europe too. However, taking into

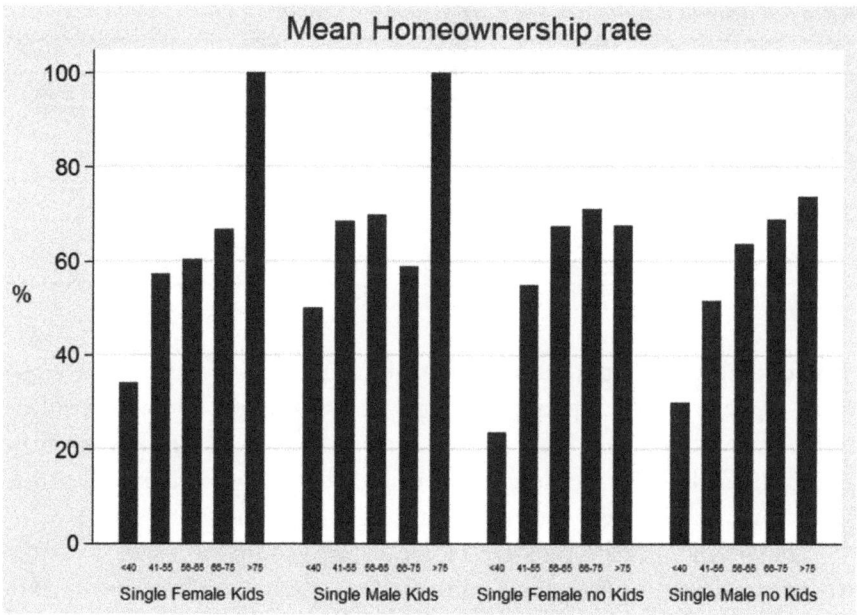

Fig. 4.1 Homeownership rate in Europe by family types

account the potential endogeneity of homeownership, the results show the opposite. Homeownership reduces the total net wealth level. The authors instrument this using inheritance, an important channel of wealth transmission, as highlighted by Piketty (2017).

Using linear regression models, we want to investigate whether the descriptive evidence shown in Table 4.1 holds when other regressors are taken into account, as shown in Table 4.2 for different household types. We regressed wealth (in log) on several explanatory variables, including homeownership. Despite not being able to claim causality, our goal is to test whether homeownership is correlated to a higher wealth level, once other variables are controlled for.

Looking at the age dimension across different types of household, we notice that the shape of accumulation is not linear but more concave, except for the people without kids for whom the accumulation process shows a more linear increase[4] (Fig. 4.2).

Table 4.2 Net Wealth regressions by country

	1	2	3	4	5	6
Variables	SFK	SMK	SFNK	SMNK	NSK	NSNK
Net wealth (log)						
Homeowner	2.80***	2.36***	2.85***	2.58***	2.07***	2.32***
Female					−0.07***	−0.26***
Age	0.05***	0.05***	0.01***	0.01***	0.04***	0.02***
Age squared	−0.08***	−0.05	0.00	−0.01	−0.03***	−0.00
University	−0.06	−0.40***	−0.02	−0.20***	−0.17***	−0.19***
University *female					0.15***	0.19***
Log total household gross income	0.69***	0.65***	0.84***	0.84***	0.83***	0.96***
Constant	0.03	1.17	0.42***	0.29	−0.42***	−0.98***
Observations	2403	464	10,923	7208	21,037	31,892
R-squared	0.55	0.48	0.55	0.53	0.54	0.58

Column 1 to 6 legend: *SFK*, single female kids; *SMK*, single male kids; *SFK*, single female kids; *SMNK*, single male no kids; *NSK*, not single with kids; *NSNK*, not single without kids
*** stands for significance at 1% level

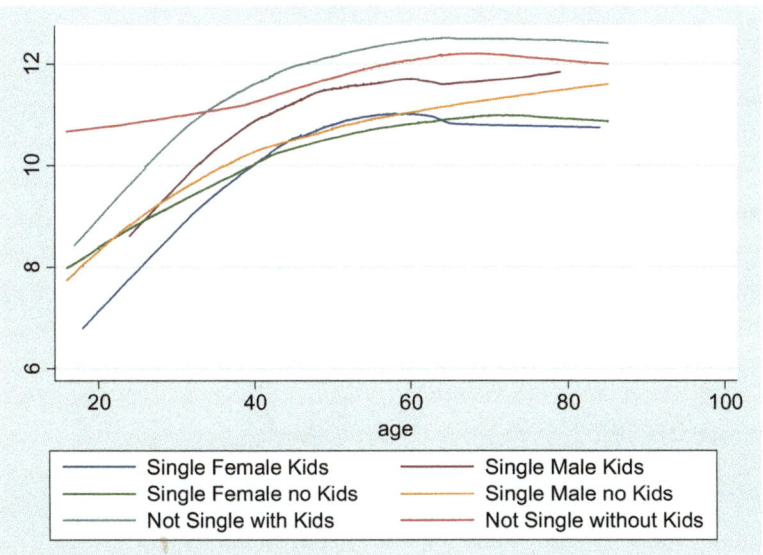

Fig. 4.2 Age and average (log) wealth by status

Our results confirm that homeownership acts as a wealth accumulating device. Households that own their home are twice as rich as households that rent their dwelling, regardless of whether they are single parents or couple households. These results are also confirmed at the country level for the whole population. Here, the homeownership impact is always positive and significant, as illustrated in Table 4.3. The effect of homeownership on wealth is at above 2 also for each country separately, as shown in Table 4.4.

Table 4.3 Net Wealth regression (pooled sample)

Variables	Wealth (1)
Homeowner	2.537***
	(0.00890)
Female	0.373***
	(0.0847)
Single-parents	−0.0580
	(0.0444)
Single-parents*female	−0.179***
	(0.0492)
Age	0.0302***
	(0.00137)
Age2	−0.000136***
	(1.31e-05)
University	0.178***
	(0.0101)
University*female	0.0424***
	(0.0155)
Individual income	0.762***
	(0.00569)
Individual income*female	−0.0509***
	(0.00806)
Employed	−0.0981***
	(0.0238)
Employed*female	0.0644**
	(0.0286)
Retired	−0.109***
	(0.0255)
Retired*female	−0.0287
	(0.0289)

(continued)

Table 4.3 (continued)

Variables	Wealth (1)
Unemployment	−0.410***
	(0.0305)
Unemployment*female	0.143***
	(0.0404)
BE	0.209***
	(0.0253)
CY	0.696***
	(0.0307)
DE	0.0166
	(0.0223)
ES	0.580***
	(0.0210)
FI	−0.375***
	(0.0195)
FR	0.203***
	(0.0189)
GR	−0.199***
	(0.0241)
IT	0.104***
	(0.0201)
LU	0.536***
	(0.0303)
NL	−0.211***
	(0.0308)
PT	−0.139***
	(0.0217)
SI	−0.107***
	(0.0295)
SK	−0.428***
	(0.0268)
Wave 2	−0.0440***
	(0.00713)
Constant	0.715***
	(0.0678)
Observations	120,501
R-squared	0.621

Austria is the country baseline
Standard errors in parentheses
***$p < 0.01$, **$p < 0.05$, *$p < 0.1$

Table 4.4 Determinants of wealth (log)

	(1)	(2)	(3)	(4)	(5)	(6)	(7)
Homeowner	2.59***	2.63***	2.26***	2.11***	2.62***	2.52***	2.49***
Female	0.00	−0.22	0.65	−0.40	1.17***	0.23	−0.38
Single	−0.18***	−0.10	−0.28**	−0.05	0.05	−0.06*	0.03
Female and single	0.10	0.08	0.07	0.11	−0.03	−0.08	−0.05
Single-parents	−0.27	−0.07	0.55*	0.01	−0.12	0.19	0.01
Single-parents × female	0.19	−0.20	−0.70*	−0.44*	−0.02	−0.25	−0.33***
Age	0.02***	0.04***	0.02***	0.01***	0.03***	0.02***	0.02***
Age squared	−0.03***	−0.03***	−0.03**	0.00	−0.01	0.01*	−0.00
University	−0.12**	−0.09*	−0.06	−0.27***	−0.07	−0.01	0.08***
University female	0.38***	0.10	0.35***	0.15**	0.10	0.12***	0.01
Log total household gross income	0.93***	0.57***	0.59***	0.92***	0.97***	0.90***	0.91***
Log total household gross income × female	−0.03	0.02	−0.07	0.00	−0.13***	−0.04	0.02
Employed	0.23	0.40***	0.36	−0.26**	0.10	−0.30***	−0.04
Employed × female	−0.11	−0.13	−0.23	0.24*	−0.06	0.08	0.11*
Retired	0.16	0.37***	0.10	−0.15	−0.05	−0.34***	−0.11**
Retired × female	−0.20	−0.31*	−0.60*	0.12	−0.10	0.07	0.12*
Unemployed	−0.53**	−0.27	0.31	−1.43***	−0.28**	−0.57***	−0.48***
Unemployed × female	0.34	0.12	−0.24	0.30	0.25	0.21**	0.16*
Second wave	−0.05	−0.17***	−0.34***	−0.02	−0.97***	0.96***	−0.64***
Constant	−0.94*	2.05***	3.58***	0.05	−1.19***	−0.80***	−0.45***
Observations	5043	4388	2341	7479	8119	16,162	24,837
R-squared	0.63	0.60	0.47	0.61	0.62	0.61	0.65
Country	Austria	Belgium	Cyprus	Germany	Spain	Finland	France

(continued)

Table 4.4 (continued)

	(8)	(9)	(10)	(11)	(12)	(13)	(14)
Homeowner	2.20***	2.71***	2.26***	2.72***	2.66***	2.62***	2.72***
Female	0.39	-0.51	0.61*	1.40***	-1.12***	0.54	-0.34
Single	0.08**	-0.06	-0.06	0.02	0.14***	-0.26**	-0.13**
Female and single	-0.06	0.01	0.03	-0.22***	0.20**	-0.33**	0.07
Single-parents	-0.16*	-0.13	0.25	-0.53***	-0.06	0.11	-0.03
Single-parents × female	-0.26**	0.04	-0.22	0.49***	-0.09	0.18	-0.04
Age	0.02***	0.01***	0.02***	0.02***	0.02***	-0.00	0.02***
Age squared	-0.01***	-0.02***	-0.03***	-0.02***	-0.02***	0.01	-0.02***
University	-0.16***	0.19***	-0.29***	0.10***	0.11***	-0.09	-0.19***
University female	0.26***	0.03	0.17***	0.12***	0.08	0.05	0.27***
Log total household gross income	0.84***	0.54***	0.71***	0.50***	0.81***	0.65***	0.35***
Log total household gross income × female	-0.05**	0.00	-0.07**	-0.16***	0.11***	-0.08	0.00
Employed	-0.13	-0.49***	0.37***	-0.17**	-0.09	-0.23	0.20*
Employed × female	0.05	0.42**	-0.23	0.30***	-0.15	0.23	0.00
Retired	-0.09	-0.53***	0.40***	-0.06	-0.12	0.08	0.10
Retired × female	-0.06	0.31*	-0.29**	0.27***	-0.24	0.08	-0.06
Unemployed	-0.35***	-0.33**	-0.38**	-0.04	-0.39***	-0.03	-0.45***
Unemployed × female	-0.02	0.06	0.57**	0.22*	0.26	0.05	0.40**
Second wave	0.26***	-0.70***	-1.33***	-0.03	0.13***	-0.43***	-0.23***
Constant	0.37**	4.08***	1.95***	3.57***	0.04	2.86***	4.51***
Observations	14,427	10,455	6733	10,137	11,580	3799	4009
R-squared	0.65	0.65	0.58	0.64	0.54	0.47	0.55
Country	Greece	Italy	Luxembourg	Netherlands	Portugal	Slovenia	Slovakia

Note: *Stands for significance at 10%, **at 5%, ***at 1%

Looking at the gender angle, we notice that being a female is significant overall and positively affects homeownership (more so than for men) on average, thus corroborating the results obtained in Rossi and Sierminska (2015) that show that women tend to accumulate more than men. Women are more inclined to wealth accumulation, a result possibly driven by a relative higher risk aversion, which, in turn, boosts savings.

4.5   Decumulation: Why Not?

In the previous section, we have shown that homeownership has a statistically significant positive effect on wealth accumulation. If accumulating resources could be seen as a good thing per se, accumulating too much could also be a cause of concern. A recent book by Reifner et al. (2010) provides an excellent review of equity release schemes all over the industrialized world. The conceptual economic framework unequivocally leads to the annuitization of wealth, in order to optimally decumulate wealth. As wealth is principally tied to housing, generating an annuity drawn upon housing assets relies on an efficient and advanced financial market that offers reverse mortgage products (Munnell et al. 2012). Despite the high potential of these products to generate annuities, empirical evidence shows that the elderly are not likely to release their housing wealth. Instead, the elderly rarely move out of their home and do not seem to consider downsizing or partially liquidating their assets to increase consumption levels. Venti and Wise (2001) show, using Health and Retirement Study data for the US, that the average older household does not liquidate housing equity to support non-housing consumption needs and conclude that most elderly families are unlikely to move.

In a summary of surveys, Turner and Yang (2006) conclude that cultural constraints to decumulation are pivotal in the process. It seems households do not behave like standard economic agents when it comes to housing decisions and thus housing equity is not necessarily considered by owners as fungible wealth. Using less strict economic lenses and recognizing that not all households necessarily act as rational economic agents, a home can be an emotional and psychological resource, particularly for older households, thus preventing them from considering their house as an asset to deplete in case of need, as would be the case with other assets

(Gibler and Rabianski 1993; Skinner 1989). These reasons make it less likely that full decumulation and annuitization will take place.

Even if there are strong motivations for little decumulation of housing equity as housing is the place where a household lives, the issue of why so little decumulation is observed in the data is still a puzzle. Since the pioneering work by Yaari (1965), the annuity puzzle has hardly been reconciled with the data. Yaari clearly shows that, when the decumulation stage takes place, most efficient individuals should subscribe to an annuity, as the return rate of an annuity is higher than that of any bond. Optimally, individuals should decumulate by annuitizing their whole asset amount.

Intuitively, the return rate of an annuity is higher than that of a bond, as it incorporates the probability of not being alive, so, if $1 + r$ will be returned in one year if one euro is invested in a bond, $(1 + r)/p$ will be returned if the same amount (one euro) is invested in an annuity type of product under a fair price, with p being the probability of being alive.[5] Despite this optimality rule, very little annuitization has been observed, and annuity subscription remains thinly spread across the population (Romiti and Rossi 2014).

As indicated by Romiti and Rossi (2014), the empirical evidence clearly shows that (elderly) households are reluctant to decumulate their assets as they age, this behavior being in contradiction to the standard life cycle theory, which predicts that households will decumulate their assets to keep their consumption smooth. In particular, their findings show that illiquid assets, such as housing wealth, which is far more difficult to liquidate, are mainly responsible for the lack of decumulation. The authors, using the SHARE (Survey of Health, Ageing, and Retirement in Europe) survey, highlight the decumulation behavior of older households in Europe by showing that financial literacy brings about more optimal behavior from a life cycle perspective. The authors examine three different dimensions of saving decisions: an unbalanced portfolio with excessive weight assigned to illiquid assets, the optimal consumption path and wealth decumulation. According to their findings, higher financial literacy substantially reduces the portfolio imbalance of people aged 50+ by reducing the weight of housing wealth in the total net worth. In addition, higher financial literacy is responsible for better consumption behavior (closer to an optimal path) and, particularly for men, for both net worth and housing wealth decumulation.

As mentioned at the beginning of this section, one of the main financial tools that helps housing equity decumulation to materialize are reverse mortgages. These allow for the transformation of housing wealth into a flow (or a lump sum) of which the current value equals that of the house at the time of death (expected). Similarly, to a standard mortgage, it is a loan with a home as collateral, but no payments are due during the life of the mortgage. Only when the owner passes away or moves to another dwelling does the bank recover the amount of the loan and the interest (Coda Moscarola et al. 2015; Dillingh et al. 2017; Toussaint 2011). The potential embedded in such instruments is very promising, as excessive illiquid housing wealth could be cashed out and by doing so increasing the living standards of the elderly. Munnell et al. (2012) argues that life cycle financial planning should include reverse mortgages as a "default." Indeed, according to economic theory households should die efficiently with a certain amount of wealth (be it zero or positive due to bequest motivations), reverse mortgages are the only instruments that make this possible. Merton (2006, 2007) highlights the potential of reverse mortgages as a buffer income to neutralize shocks due to pension risk (Bodie 2012) and as a device to make the timing of bequests more efficient and the magnitude of bequest close to the desired one rather than being unplanned.

4.6 Possible Dangers of Excessively High Homeownership Levels

The ability to accumulate wealth certainly translates into financial stability for households (Romiti and Rossi 2014). A buffer stock of wealth reduces households' vulnerability to bad shock realizations, thus representing a crucial factor of financial protection. As housing is the main form of wealth, does housing wealth reduce the risk of financial vulnerability? Actually, there seems to be a threshold above which housing wealth can represent a source of vulnerability rather than the other way around. In this vein, Brunetti et al. (2016) show that there is a link between an illiquid household portfolio and the financial fragility of the household, which they define as having insufficient liquid assets to cope with unexpected expenses. Their main findings are that, in addition to standard demographic factors, such as financial literacy (education), gender, wealth and employment status, homeownership plays an important role in increasing the likelihood of being financially fragile, particularly among the elderly. Summing up the existing evidence, homeownership can certainly help households to step on to the wealth escalator, but a warning about excessive illiquidity is also of concern, particularly in the face of consistently high levels of housing equity compared with annual income levels.

Oswald (1996) conjectures that the high unemployment rate of the Western economies has been encouraged by the pace of increase in homeownership. The author shows that the derivative of homeownership on unemployment (du/dh) is always positive. His calculations based on evidence from developed nations—the US, the UK, Italy, France and Sweden—albeit tentative, show that a 10 percentage point increase in homeownership is associated with an increase of approximately 2 percentage points in the unemployment rate.

Following this argument, we can conjecture that governmental policies of Western countries oriented toward a stable increase in homeownership might inadvertently have worsened the efficiency of labor markets. Unemployment is inversely related to job search effort, and homeownership in turn might affect job search intensity, probably in a negative direction. Owning is, in other words, likely to reduce individuals' mobility and thus boost unemployment.

At the macro level, a clear pattern emerges empirically. Homeownership is correlated with unemployment, suggesting that a more prudential approach should be considered when promoting homeownership at the government level as a neutral or pro-growth policy.

4.7 Conclusions

In this chapter, we provide evidence on homeownership as a possible wealth escalator at the European and American levels. Empirical results unequivocally show that homeownership is associated with higher values of wealth. Moreover, women tend to show a higher propensity for accumulation, which makes women, in the long run, less exposed to the risk of running out of assets. In fact, homeownership for women could be seen as a stronger tool for accumulation than for men. This can be particularly important after retirement given their longer life expectancy.

We also argue that a more prudential approach should be taken when considering homeownership with a positive connotation only. Indeed, at the micro level, homeowners do show higher levels of wealth. However, this could come at a cost. Homeowners could cause lower mobility and a lower effort in job searching, which, in the long run, could lead to lower growth and more pronounced unemployment (as highlighted by Oswald 1996). Given all the empirical evidence collected, it seems that, after a certain threshold, homeownership can become a cause of real policy concern, causing, for instance, financial fragility.

Notes

1. There is a mountain of research discussing the relationship between homeownership and labor markets and voluminous one pointing to the fact that homeowners have better employment outcomes. See Morescalchi (2016) for a review.
2. There have been numerous attempts to examine the causality of this link, which is extremely complicated, particularly if homeownership is examined within portfolio choices. Most recently Beracha et al. found that homeownership improves wealth creation on a risk-adjusted basis as a part of the household portfolio. Renters may achieve higher returns, but not in very realistic scenarios.
3. Assets can be summarized as a composite bundle of activities and liabilities and are a rather non-homogeneous stock. Net assets represent the sum of financial wealth made up of risky (stocks) and less risky assets (bonds) and real wealth (housing equities) minus debts, including mortgages on housing.
4. If the data are cross-sectional, the age effect could be wrongly interpreted as mixing a cohort effect, as shown conceptually in the seminal paper by Shorrocks (1975). However, the U-shaped age effect is also found using panel data by Romiti and Rossi (2014).
5. See Yaari (1965) and more recently Lockwood (2012).

Bibliography

Belsky, E., & Prakken, J. (2004). *Housing wealth effects: Housing's impact on wealth accumulation, wealth distribution and consumer spending*. Working Paper, W04-13, Joint Center for Housing Studies, Harvard University, Cambridge.

Bodie, Z. (2012). *The safety first approach to investing, key note speech*. Conference on Pension Risk Management, Free University, March 15, Amsterdam.

Bokhari, S., Torous, W., & Wheaton, W. (2013). *Why did household mortgage leverage rise from the mid-1980s until the great recession?* In American Economic Association 2013 Annual Meeting. San Diego, California.

Borella, M., & Rossi, M. (2014). *Asset accumulation and decumulation over the life cycle*. Netspar Panel Paper 39.

Borella, M., Moscarola, F. C., & Rossi, M. (2014). (Un)expected retirement and the consumption puzzle. *Empirical Economics, 47*(2), 733–751.

Brunetti, M., Giarda, E., & Torricelli, C. (2016). Is financial fragility a matter of illiquidity? An appraisal for Italian households. *Review of Income and Wealth, 62*, 628–649.

Calcagno, R., Fornero, E., & Rossi, M. C. (2009). The effect of house prices on household consumption in Italy. *Journal of Real Estate Finance and Economics, 39*(3), 284–300.

Chiuri, M. C., & Jappelli, T. (2010). Do the elderly reduce housing equity? An international comparison. *Journal of Population Economics, 23*(2), 643–663.

Coda Moscarola, F., D'Addio, A. C., Fornero, E., & Rossi, M. (2015). Reverse mortgage: A tool to reduce old age poverty without sacrificing social inclusion. In A. Börsch-Supan, T. Kneip, H. Litwin, M. Myck, & G. Weber (Eds.), *Ageing in Europe—Supporting policies for an inclusive society* (pp. 235–244). De Gruyter.

Deaton, A. (1992). *Understanding consumption*. Cambridge: Cambridge University Press.

Dillingh, R., Prast, H., Rossi, M., & Brancati, C. U. (2017). Who wants to have their home and eat it too? Interest in reverse mortgages in the Netherlands. *Journal of Housing Economics, 38*, 25–37.

Elsinga, M., Quilgars, D., & Doling, J. (2012). Where housing and pensions meet. *International Journal of Housing Policy, 12*(1), 1–12.

Friedman, M. (1957). *A theory of the consumption function*. Princeton: Princeton University Press.

Gibler, K. M., & Rabianski, J. (1993). Elderly interest in home equity conversion. *Housing Policy Debate, 4*(4), 565–588.

Goodman, L. S., & Mayer, C. (2018). Homeownership and the American dream. *Journal of Economic Perspectives, 32*(1), 31–58.

Horsewood N., & Neuteboom, P. (2006). *The social limits to growth: Security and insecurity aspects of home ownership* (Vol. 31). IOS Press.

Kaas, L., Kocharkov, G., & Preugschat, E. (2016). *Does homeownership promote wealth accumulation?* University of Konstanz Department of Economics, Working Paper Series 2016-03.

Laibson, D. (1997). Golden eggs and hyperbolic discounting. *Quarterly Journal of Economics, 112*, 443–477.

Li, W., & Yang, F. (2010). American dream or American obsession? *Business Review (Federal Reserve Bank of Philadelphia)*, 20–30.

Lockwood, L. M. (2012). Bequest motives and the annuity puzzle. *Review of Economic Dynamics, 15*(2), 226–243.

Merton, R. C. (2006). Observations on innovation in pension fund management in the impending future. *PREA Quarterly*, Winter, 61–67.

Merton, R. C. (2007). *The future of retirement planning.* CFA Research Institute.

Mitchell, O. S., Poterba, J. M., Warshawsky, M. J., & Brown, J. R. (1999). New evidence on the money's worth of individual annuities. *American Economic Review, 89*(5), 1299–1318.

Modigliani, F., & Brumberg, R. (1954). Utility analysis and the consumption function. In K. K. Kurihara (Ed.), *Post-Keynesian ecnomics* (pp. 17–42). London: Allen & Unwin.

Morescalchi, A. (2016). The puzzle of job search and housing tenure: A reconciliation of theory and empirical evidence. *Journal of Regional Science, 56*(2), 288–312.

Munnell, A. H., Orlova, N., & Webb, A. (2012). *How important is asset allocation to financial security in retirement?* Center for Retirement Research at Boston College Working Paper No. 2012-13. Retrieved from SSRN http://ssrn.com/abstract=2039385.

Oswald, A. J. (1996). *A conjecture on the explanation for high unemployment in the industrialized nations: Part 1.* Working Paper. Coventry: University of Warwick, Department of Economics. Warwick Economic Research Papers (No. 475).

Piketty, T. (2017). *Capital in the twenty-first century.* Harvard: Harvard University Press.

Reifner, U., Clerc-Renaud, S., Pérez-Carillo, E., & Tiffe, A. (2010). *Equity release schemes in the European Union.* Norderstedt: Books on Demand.

Romiti, A., & Rossi, M. (2014). Housing wealth decumulation, portfolio composition and financial literacy among European elderly. Carlo Alberto Notebooks 375, Collegio Carlo Alberto.

Rossi, M. & Sierminska, E. (2015). *Single again? Saving patterns when widowhood occurs.* Netspar Discussion Paper No. 02/2015-004. https://doi.org/10.2139/ssrn.2569127.

Schlafmann, K. (2016). *Housing, mortgages, and self control.* CEPR Discussion Papers 11589, C.E.P.R. Discussion Papers.

Shiller, R. (2007). *Understanding recent trends in house prices and homeowneship.* NBER working paper #13553.

Shorrocks, A. F. (1975). The age-wealth relationship a cross-section and cohort analysis. *The Review of Economics and Statistics, 57,* 155–163.

Sierminska, E. (2018). The 'wealth-being' of single parents. In L. Maldonado & R. Nieuwenhuis (Eds.), *The triple bind of single-parent families,* Chapter 13. Policy Press.

Sinai, T., & Souleles, N. S. (2005). Owner-occupied housing as a hedge against rent risk. *The Quarterly Journal of Economics, 120*(2), 763–789.

Skinner, J. (1989). Housing wealth and aggregate saving. *Regional Science and Urban Economics, 19*(2), 305–324.

Takhtamanova, Y., & Sierminska, E. (2012). Financial and housing wealth and consumption spending: Cross country and age group comparisons. *Housing Studies, 27*(5), 685–719.

Toussaint, J. (2011). Housing assets as a potential solution for financial hardship: Households' mental accounts of housing wealth in three European countries. *Housing, Theory and Society, 28*(4), 320–341.

Turner, B., & Yang, Z. (2006). Security of home ownership–using equity or benefiting from low debt? *International Journal of Housing Policy, 6*(3), 279–296.

Usatoday Newspaper. (2014, September 14). Retrieved from https://www.usatoday.com/story/money/personalfinance/2014/05/10/why-your-home-is-not-a-good-investment/8900911/.

Van der Schors, A., Alessie, R., & Mastrogiacomo, M. (2007). *Home and mortgage ownership of the Dutch elderly; explaining cohort, time and age effects* (No. 77). CPB Netherlands Bureau for Economic Policy Analysis.

Van Rooij, M. C., Lusardi, A., & Alessie, R. J. (2012). Financial literacy, retirement planning and household wealth. *The Economic Journal, 122*(560), 449–478.

Venti F., & Wise, D. A. (2001). Choice, chance, and wealth dispersion at retirement. NBER Chapters. In *Aging issues in the United States and Japan* (pp. 25–64). National Bureau of Economic Research, Inc.

Warshawsky, M. J. (2018). Retire on the House: The Possible Use of Reverse Mortgages to Enhance Retirement Security. *The Journal of Retirement Winter*, 5(3), 10–31.

Yaari, M. (1965). Uncertain lifetime, life insurance and the theory of the consumer. *Review of Economics Studies, 32*, 137–150.

Concluding Remarks

In this book, we have drawn the economic framework within which to insert the complex household decision to consume and save, by accumulating wealth. We, then, moved to carry out an empirical analysis across OECD countries to investigate the determinants of homeownership and wealth across different household types, showing that single households with kids have a more vulnerable status than married households. We provide suggestive evidence that homeownership and wealth go hand in hand, with homeowners being richer than renters across all countries. Despite this strong evidence, we cannot claim the link to be causal, due to the propensity for accumulation characterizing each household in a different way (not just in terms of homeownership, but the whole household portfolio), and likely to drive the correlation between homeownership and wealth. Further investigations on the causal link between homeownership and wealth seem to be very important for future agenda setting and for designing sound welfare policies, often advocating homeownership as one of the necessary ingredients for reducing vulnerability without looking at the potential drawback of "excessively high" homeownership rates and for closing the gender wealth gap.

© The Author(s) 2018
M. Rossi, E. M. Sierminska, *Wealth and Homeownership*,
https://doi.org/10.1007/978-3-319-92558-5

Policies that take into account the specific needs and barriers of families and single parents (whether they are women or men) in particular would need to be developed (Sierminska 2018). Building up wealth on housing seems an important step to reduce household vulnerability to shocks and to accumulate a buffer stock of wealth; however, we want to point out to the reader that housing wealth should be taken with prudence as an excessive illiquid portfolio could represent a source of vulnerability per se. This vulnerability can even be stronger if financial markets offer limited possibilities of financial products that allow housing decumulation in old age. If households overinvest in housing and have little possibilities to drawn on their wealth, this makes them vulnerable to lack of liquid wealth when needed (Dillingh et al. 2017).

Women show less vulnerability in wealth holdings than what a simple wealth gap would suggest, particularly in Europe. Indeed, diving into the determinants of wealth accumulation and controlling for other explanatory variables, we show that women have a higher propensity to save and they show higher wealth levels. The propensity to consume and save across different forms of saving products across genders is also an interesting and promising research topic that has not been intensively explored in academic research.

Bibliography

Dillingh, R., Prast, H., Rossi, M., & Brancati, C. U. (2017). Who wants to have their home and eat it too? Interest in reverse mortgages in the Netherlands. *Journal of Housing Economics, 38*, 25–37.

Sierminska, E. (2018). The 'wealth-being' of single parents, Chapter 13. In L. Maldonado & R. Nieuwenhuis (Eds.), *The triple bind of single-parent families*. Policy Press.

Index

A

Accumulation, 22, 45
Affordability, 38
Annuitization of wealth, 108
Annuity puzzle, 109
Arbitrage, 101
Asset, 14

B

Behavioral economics, 96
Bequests, 13, 100
Borrow, 8
Borrowing restrictions, 11
Buffer stock, 14

C

Cohorts, 71
Commitment to save, 3

Community property regimes, 24
Composite good, 43
Consumption, 94, 97
Costs for mobility, 98
Cross-country comparisons, 46

D

Debt anchor, 25
Decumulation, 13, 97, 99
Dissaving, 9, 98
Divorced, 33
Downsizing, 108
Dwelling, 12

E

Economic vulnerability, 44
Economic well-being, 20, 57

Education, 21
Endogeneity, 96, 101

F

Families, 28–30
Family type, 28, 33, 36–38, 47–49
Financial assets, 46
Financial awareness, 100
Financial crisis, 96
Financial instability, 5
Financial literacy, 99, 109
Financial planning, 4
Financial vulnerability, 110
First pillar, 56
Fringe benefits, 25
Fungible wealth, 108

G

Gender, 4, 108
Gender wealth gap, 22

H

Habits, 2, 6
Home equity, 38, 57
Homeownership, 38, 42, 101, 102
  gaps, 59
  rates, 60
Household budget, 5
Household Finance and
  Consumption Survey (HFCS),
  48, 100
Household structure, 62
House price, 45
Housing, 38, 43
  equity, 2, 13
  service, 12
  tenure, 96
  wealth, 93

I

Illiquid, 5, 44, 111
Indebtedness, 6
Inheritance, 7, 102
Institutions, 27
Interest rate, 10

J

Job search, 111

L

Labor market, 25–26, 94
Legal system, 23
Leisure, 6
Life cycle model, 6, 24, 47
Life cycle permanent
  income model
  (LCPI), 13, 97
Life event, 4
Liquid, 40
Liquidity constrained, 40
Luxembourg Income Study
  (LIS) Database, 47,
  58
Luxembourg Wealth Study (LWS)
  Database, 47

M

Married, 35
Married couple, 65

Men, 5
Mortality rates, 23
Mortgage, 96, 98
Mortgage market, 28
Myopia, 96

N

Never married, 29
Non-monetary return, 6

O

Over accumulation, 94
Owned outright, 40
Owner-occupied housing, 21

P

Parsimonious, 2
Pension risk, 110
Pension system, 10
Pension wealth, 2, 10
Permanent, 7
Ponzi games, 97
Portfolio, 5
Post-communist countries, 61
Precautionary motives, 11
Probit, 65
Property ladder, 66

R

Regression, 101
Renters, 101
Renting, 3
Retirement, 22, 97
Reverse, 99

Reverse mortgages, 110
Risk, 24, 43
Risk-averse, 58

S

Saving propensity, 2
Saving rate, 11
Savings, 8
Self-control, 96
SHARE, 109
Single households, 62
Single men, 56, 65
Single parent, 29, 35, 45
Single-person households, 23
Single women, 56, 66, 101
Smooth consumption, 44
Smoothing, 97
Spouses, 5
Standard of living, 20

T

Tax, 44
Tax laws, 28
Time trend, 73
Timing of house purchases, 94

U

Unemployment, 57, 94, 111
Unexpected expenses, 111
Unintended, 100
Utility, 97

V

Vulnerability, 8

W

Wealth, 20, 46
   accumulation, 4, 13
   escalator, 25
   gap, 96
   inequality, 3
   transmission, 102
Well-being, 6, 13
Women, 5
Work tenure, 71

CPSIA information can be obtained
at www.ICGtesting.com
Printed in the USA
BVHW020251281119
565074BV00010B/245/P